Understanding ɑ
Suicidal Thought

Surviving Narcissistic
Parenting

Stephen Broughton

chipmunkapublishing
the mental health publisher

Published by
Chipmunkapublishing
PO Box 6872
Brentwood
Essex CM13 1ZT
United Kingdom

http://www.chipmunkapublishing.com

ISBN 978-1-84991-729-2

Chipmunkapublishing gratefully acknowledge the support of Arts Council England.

Helen

Most Wonderful Wife

Harriet Chloe Joe And Lily

Best Family

And Dick....Not So Bad After All

I Love You All

X

Little Dick

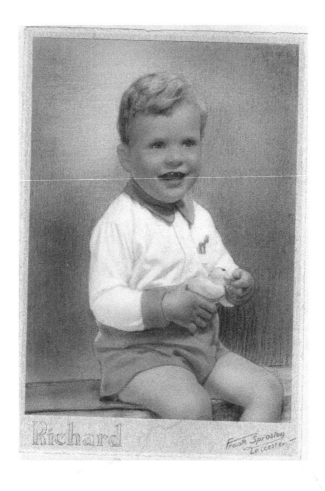

CHAPTER ONE BEGINNINGS

We all dream and we probably dream every night. But have you ever wondered why we only remember some of the dreams and the others are consigned to some cerebral recycle bin? And why we sometimes have the same dream over and over again?

I have had, for so long as I have known, a dream where I suddenly discover that I have a house. A tiny derelict house with an over grown garden. Hidden away with no proper path to it. And when I look at the house I see that there's so much work to be done to make it into a place to live, that I know it's beyond me and that makes me very sad.

And there's another dream where I've killed someone a long time ago and nobody but me knows and I'm afraid that someone will some day find out the terrible thing that I have done. And I wake up believing the dream is true, not knowing how I can live with myself having done the terrible thing that I have done.

So this book is about how I found out about the person I might have killed and how I first found and then set about rebuilding the house that was nothing but an empty shell with a gaping hole in the roof.

And have you ever wondered why we have the memories of our childhood that we have? Sometimes trivial every day memories. Like a video running in our mind which never got erased by the other trivial every day memories that we record each day.

I have always remembered as if it was yesterday, the day when a white van drew up outside our house and a man in a white coat got out. Our dog was a corgi we called Lightie. The man came into our living room. Lightie was behind the sofa and he picked her up in his arms and took her away. And I never knew why I remembered that so well. Many years later when I had gone past the age they call middle age I told my Mother about that memory. She was amazed at what I said, because she said I could only have been about 12 months at the time. I had just started to walk and the dog was getting old and no longer as reliable as it needed to be with a toddler around.

This is a picture of me and my Mother and Lightie. I was more interested in the dog than in my Mother or whoever was taking the photo. Presumably, my Father.

And I remembered as well being in bed with my parents one Sunday morning. They had a cup of tea and there was a tin of biscuits and I said to my Mother, 'I know what I want to be when I grow up,' 'I want to be a sheep farmer in New Zealand.' And she said to me. 'Oh, you wouldn't leave me would you?' And why should I remember that?

And I always wanted to write a book and I doubted that I ever would. I thought nobody would ever read it even if I did, and you have now proved me wrong.

I took up running and when I first started, a mile seemed a very long way and before long I had run a half marathon, 13.1 miles and that didn't seem too difficult so I ran a full marathon 26.2 miles and that didn't seem too difficult. So I ran another marathon and another and endless half marathons and that didn't seem too difficult and now I've been running for nearly 20 years and that hasn't been too difficult so maybe I could write a book and maybe I've now done the most difficult part.

Like running, the most difficult part is getting started. And I've done that now so maybe I could rebuild that house now that I've started and maybe I could find out whether I had killed that person. And by the time I've finished I'll know why I remember those things and it will all start to make sense. But it could take a long time to find out and this is the story of how one person discovered what had happened, to make him like he was. And why every day he wished he was dead and how he tried to find a reason to live. How he hoped that one day he would have a day when he didn't wish he was dead. That maybe this might help you understand who you are, and why you are the way you are and what made you like that. And whether life could be just a little bit better.

A story always starts at where the writer thinks there's a beginning. But the beginning of this story is lost. It all happened such a very long time ago. There was a sign of what might have been. By the back door of my Grandmother's house in Tresham Street in Kettering was a place in the wall where the plaster had been repaired. My Mother told me that one day, when she was young, she took a hammer and smashed it against the wall. The plaster fell away leaving a huge hole. It was repaired but you can never rub out the mark between the old and the new. 'I was that mad.' She said. But I never knew what she was mad about. And maybe 'mad' was exactly what she was and always had been.

I imagine that you have been that angry. Angry enough to take a hammer and smash it against the wall. Most people have and I know I must have been that angry too but try as I might I've never been able to let the anger out. I've never been able to stamp my feet. Shout. Swear or do all the many things people do when they're mad. No, when I get angry the anger has nowhere to go except back to where it came from. I find it hard to even remember being angry. I only remember being sad and defeated by it all. Can you imagine a life where you can only turn your anger against yourself and you end up wishing you were dead? Not sometimes, occasionally, on a bad day. But every day. Because you had a mother who was so obsessed with her own anger that she didn't notice her child. Like the babies who never cry because no one comes when they cry. No one noticed when I was upset so I never cried out for help, and I still can't. Not even to ask for a cup of tea. You never say what you feel. You don't feel. You never bash a wall with a hammer. You never think your feelings matter. So you just die. You become an empty shell with a hole in the roof with no path to take you there. And you don't leave a mark on the wall. You just sink like a stone in a pond with barely a ripple to show where you drowned. And the person that was you, lies dead.

I shall never know what made my Mother so angry. She loved her Father and he loved her. It was her Mother that made her angry. But why, I shall never know. So this book starts half way through the story but by the end perhaps we shall both understand more of the whys and hows.

Life in Kettering is where I shall begin.

My Grand Parents' world was like a window onto Edwardian England. I suppose one day my grandchildren will feel the same about my world. But the Edwardian era was one of great hardship and discomfort. Baths with no hot water. Water was heated in a copper in the kitchen and carried upstairs in buckets. The copper was a brick structure in the corner of the kitchen and in the centre was a metal bowl into which water was poured. Underneath was a coal fire and when I was due a bath I was placed in the metal bowl with a roaring fire beneath and immersed in it like a missionary cooking for the cannibals. The toilet was outside in the yard with pieces of torn up newspaper if you needed it. And until you did you always had something to read, though you never got the whole story. In the yard were the hens, guarded by the cockerel. So a visit to the toilet meant running the gauntlet of the cockerel and the hens. The cockerel attacked me one day pecking my legs but only the once. After that I was on the alert and made sure the cockerel was busy somewhere else.

The yard was a magical playground for a young lad. There were a series of garages, which were hired to people to house a motorbike or small car. There was one stable for Mr. Abraham's horse. He was a fishmonger. Fish was 6d and chips 2d. At the bottom of the yard was a workshop where light industrial work was carried out. My Grandmother's Father was a carpenter by trade and hand made the staircase there. I loved watching the men at their lathes. There were amazing piles of swarf, the bits the lathes cut off all curled in silvery spirals. In one of the garages was my Grandad's motorbike and sidecar. An 'Indian.' An American imported bike, which was just magnificent to behold. 7.9 horsepower with carbide lighting. The first time my Grandad started it up he went straight across the road into the house opposite. No damage done

My Grandmother was carried in the sidecar and when she was little my Mother was wedged between her legs, sitting on a petrol can with a cushion. The sidecar was open to the elements and if it rained hard they would shelter under a bridge. In a sidecar you had to 'lean over' going round corners and we continued the tradition even when we had a car. Every bank holiday they would travel in the motorbike and sidecar from Kettering to Devon to see Grandad's family. Quite a journey with roads as they were then.

My Mother took us to Kettering most Saturdays. The journey to Kettering was a great treat. Motoring was something new and exciting in those days. A real adventure. The roads twisted and turned and you rarely saw another car. On the way back we would sometimes stop at what was called an 'outdoor beerhouse' or off-license as we would call it now for a bottle of 'pop' (fizzy drink) and some sweets.

The kitchen sink in my Grandmother's kitchen had one cold water tap, which was rarely used but it had a pump handle to draw water from a well. An indoor pump handle was quite a 'mod con.' It was lovely soft water, so cold in summer. There was no cooker, just a range with a coal fire and a hook to hang your pans from. There was no fridge, just a cold slab in the pantry and a meat safe to keep the flies off. There was no TV. No alcohol. No drinks with your meal. No swearing. No kindness, except from my Grandad who taught me to box.

The kitchen made do as a sitting room. There was a large wooden table in the centre and the cutlery was kept in the draws. There were about 6 grandfather clocks in their kitchen but I can't remember any telling the time.

They had a sitting room 'upstairs' but it was never used. In it was a magnificent wind up gramophone, which I loved to play. Before I could walk I could put a record on and listen to the music, songs like 'The Laughing Policeman' and 'The Teddy Bears Picnic.' 'If you go down to the woods today you're sure of a big surprise.'

There was a downstairs drawing room but all the chairs were covered in 'stock' for the shop. Great piles of vests, pants and jeans all wrapped in brown paper and string. Before central heating, everyone wore a vest, aertex in the summer, woolly 'chilpruffe' ones in the winter and pants to match. There were at least four pianos in this room, but only one was used. Nanna was a piano teacher. It was all 'doh re me' and 'do te la me so.' This was called the 'tonic sol fa' scale. Those familiar with 'The Sound of Music' will know how it works.

The house was next door to a shoe factory. In those days there was hardly anywhere in Kettering that wasn't near a shoe factory. The shoe factory had a brass band, which used to practice and practice. I learned to love listening to the band practice. I would sit in the yard listening to them start, start again and again until they eventually got it right. When you hear music played by a brass band you have little idea of the amazing amount of work which goes in to making it perfect. It's the only form of music where the top performers set themselves in competion with each other on an annual basis to see who plays the best. The judges sit under the stage so they can hear the performance but can't see which band is giving it.

My Grandfather was the youngest son of 14 children born in the 21 years following his parents' marriage in 1867. The first 9 children were born in the space of the first 10 years. Grandma Hancock slowed down a bit after that! His Father and Grandfather were both drunkards. His Grandmother promised his Grandfather that if he ever returned home drunk on market day again she wouldn't let him in. One day he did, and she didn't and he was left to sleep it off by the locked front door. He caught pneumonia and within a few days he died. When asked if she felt sorry for what she'd done she said simply, "No, I said I would do it and I did." She later remarried.

His own Mother wasn't so lucky. Needing money to buy food for her 14 children and no help from a drunken husband she would walk to Tiverton to beg from her own Mother who was a wealthy Mill owner. Eventually her Mother said, "no more," and it broke her spirit. She struggled home in the heat that hot summers day and 'took a chill,' and died. My Grandad was 7 years old and he and his 3-year-old sister Dot, went to live with their Uncle Jonas, a farmer at Stag Mill Uplowman near Tiverton. Every morning from the age of 7 he had to milk six cows, walk three miles to school, and then at the end of the day walk home and milk six cows again. Bear in mind that it can take twenty minutes to milk one cow and before you could milk them you had to bring them in from the fields! Living on a farm he was fed well but he would give his packed lunch to the poor children at the school who had none. They were known as 'boarders' but I don't know why. Perhaps they were homeless orphans paid for by the School Board.

Many years later, Auntie Dot's son Dennis turned up at our house in Leicester begging for food and money. He too was an alcoholic.

At the age of 12 Grandad was sent to Western super Mare to be apprenticed as an Ironmonger. He eventually set himself up in business in Kettering as an Ironmonger in partnership with a man who was a churchwarden. The man robbed him of his money and the business failed. After that he never again went to Church. He then set himself up as a Gent's outfitters. His customers were the workers at the shoe factories buying their work clothes, their trousers, shirts and even their boots.

Alongside the clothing business, with a separate entrance in the yard at the side was his Pawnbroking business. There was a stigma attached to the customers being driven by poverty to use a Pawn shop and to the pawnbroker himself, similar to 'porn' today. We're now ashamed of sex. In those days people were ashamed of poverty. Yet society couldn't function without the pawnbroker. There was no other credit and for many pawning your Sunday suit was the only way to put food on the table until payday came.

If the world was Edwardian the characters were Dickensian. My Mother had 2 Aunts. Kate and Aunt Flo. Aunt Flo was a cripple. When she was 8 years old her Father pushed her over and she broke her back on the brass rail, which went round the fireplace. She never grew after that and was never able to walk without crutches. Her Father put her in a horse and trap to take her to Northampton Hospital and the journey was a terrible agony. The Doctors didn't do much good in those days.

To know my Grandfather's story was to know the evils of drink and even today maybe 100 years later I wouldn't risk 'one too many.' It was the same with gambling. Playing cards were the work of the devil and never allowed although in her later years my Mother did allow herself to play Patience!

My Grandmother's birth certificate records the wrong date. Her Father got drunk celebrating her birth and by the time he stopped celebrating several days later he'd forgotten the date she was born. Her name was Lizzie. My Mother once said to me,' If ever I get like my Mother you must tell me.' It was too late. She was so like her Mother and always had been.

My Aunt Kate told the story of how she had an operation to save her eyesight when she was a little girl. The Surgeon came to the house and operated on the kitchen table. There was no anaesthetic just a sip or two of brandy. She told me with a sort of pride that her screams could be heard in the next street. 'The Doctor said I'd been so good he gave me a little dolly'.

Kate and Flo never married. They belonged to a generation where the men were lost on the Somme or some similar killing field. 750,000 of them. Their house was next door to the Kettering Working Men's club where Kate spent most of her evenings. This was unheard of for a woman to go drinking but she was an exception. The family all smelled of snuff. Snuff was a tobacco powder that people sniffed from the side of their index finger. I used to go to the Outdoor Beer House to get the snuff. It was weighed out on a set of brass scales into a conical shaped paper bag. It was kept in a snuffbox.

Aunt Flo loved going in the car for a ride. It's what people did in those days when the roads were empty and travel something new. To Flo, everything she saw was new and wonderful. No matter how many times she had been there, seen that, it made her excited like a little child. My Mother took her out one day and she saw what she thought was a wonderful hotel, 'I wish I could go there one day,' said Flo. 'You will one day,' said my Mother. It was the Kettering Crematorium.

One day Kate was having a drink in the club and she took out of her bag a small tube of laxatives. Thinking they were sweets a man asked if he could have one. Then another. Kate said he could have the packet, which he did. For many years thereafter the family enjoyed the story of how loose the man was the next day and still not knowing what he'd eaten.

My Mother adored her Father and he adored her. My Grandmother was an unpleasant person. We all knew from an early age that Nanna was an LRAM. A Liscenciate of the Royal Academy of Music. Like the highest level of music you could aspire to without being Sir John Barbiroli or Edward Elgar. She played the piano and was the organist at St Mary's Church, the main Church in Kettering. She gave music lessons to the people of Kettering. The pupil would be playing in the downstairs sitting room and Nanna would be sitting in the kitchen with us. In mid sentence she would break off to hurl some instruction to the frightened pupil who would try again and again and again till he or she got it right.

But my Mother never got it quite right. She played well, sang well and played the violin in an Orchestra but was never praised and never given credit.

She treated me the same and justified it by saying that she couldn't praise me, or indeed any one, because her Mother never praised her. That was part of her anger. I still have her violin. I always thought it would be valuable but it isn't. It came out of the pledge office, like many things in our family. Second hand, used and abandoned.

She had been a sickly child suffering from Diphtheria. She described it like this, "I had to go to the fever Hospital in Rockingham Road. I remember seeing my Mother and Dad through the windows, they weren't allowed in to see me. Remember demanding red jelly, refused to eat yellow jelly. I could see they had red in the other ward. Poorly for a long time after. Had to go to school in a pram, (a wicker one). Was given cocoa for elevenses at school, the only child in the school to have this. Made by caretaker." She was 5 years old when this happened. The words were written 70 years later and you can feel the anger still burning fiercely.

Every summer after getting Diphtheria she was sent away to the country. The Doctors in those days were very keen on sunshine and fresh air as a cure for serious illness. My Grandfather had endless numbers of brothers and sisters dotted around the country who would look after her. Allegedly they had each been given a thousand pounds to set themselves up in business following the death of his Grandmother Mary Wood the Mill owner in Devon. The most notable member of my Grandfather's family was my Mother's Aunt Edith who lived near Lowestoft. She had married a Baker and between them they had built up a vast empire of café's, restaurants and hotels. Purdy's cafes were as well known in East Anglia, as Lyons Corner Houses were in London. They belonged to an age when Ladies ceased work upon marrying and spent their days with domestic chores and shopping. In the afternoons Ladies would 'take tea' with a plate of cakes and Purdy's made a fortune in the process. My Great Uncle invented a way of putting fruitcakes into tins so they could be sent around the world as presents and kept fresh till they were opened.

Aunt Edith's tragedy was that she only had daughters. The daughters married and their respective husbands eventually ran the business. According to my Mother they caused it to collapse by expanding into hotels and the fortune was lost in the process. More anger that she didn't inherit or benefit by a single penny from their wealth but then why should she? I was once taken to see Aunt Edith. We were given tea and cakes but she couldn't quite understand why we had traveled halfway across the Country, just to see her and without telling her we were going. My Mother always assumed people would be delighted to see her!

My Grandfather bought a small house in the Northants village of Stoke Albany for his retirement. We sometimes went to see it. It was derelict. Now I think of it, maybe my dream came about because of this house. Somehow the house was rebuilt and Tenants found for it. When my Grandfather died my Mother expected to inherit the house but he left it to my Grandmother. More anger.

Being tenanted it became worthless because of the Rent Acts. When eventually it was sold to the Tenants it fetched very little. The Tenants sold it a few days later and made a great deal of money. More anger. It's funny how a similar thing happened to my Father's Grandfather. When he died, death duties had to be paid. Soon after, his house was compulsorily purchased for road widening and the family ended up receiving less in compensation than they had paid in death duties. More anger. It was a lovely house too. Built of stone. It was across the road from my primary school and there is now a library on the site.

The greatest tragedy which made my Mother really, really angry was the First World War. I suppose it made a lot of people pretty angry too. It also made them fatherless husband less and child less, none of which happened to my Mother. I will have to tell you the story of my Mothers cousin Raymond if I remember to. That made her pretty angry too. People were never angry with the Germans. They just hated the Upper Class twits, the officers, the politicians, who led them to such a futile slaughter.

My Grandad was a 'consci.' A conscientious objector, a man who refused to go to war. In the modern world we can't imagine the hatred and loathing that people had for conscis. They were pathetic cowards who would let others give their lives whilst they stayed behind cowering. To me he was a very strong and powerful man or so it seemed to me as a little boy.

Actually, maybe now is the time to tell you about Raymond because his story shows a lot about War and the effect on ordinary people. Raymond was called up to be a Tank driver in the Second War. After a few weeks basic training he was sent to battle in France. On his first day his Tank was blown up and that was the end of Raymond apart from a few faded photographs of the proud young man in his new uniform and a letter he wrote to my

Mother which I treasure. I always felt sorry for Raymond even though he died before I was born. Such was the anger that was felt at his sad loss. To my Mother and to you too I suppose, it shows the futility of War. Nobody who went to War thought it was anything but totally futile. But the story of Raymond was used to show how my Grandad was right and the rest of the world was wrong. After the war he was asked to stand as MP for Kettering but he refused believing that politicians were what was wrong with the Country. I dare say that many now would have sympathy with that point of view.

Being ahead of your time was no great comfort as he was taken off to Wormwood Scrubs to serve his punishment. I wonder if they would have had more sympathy if he was a Pacifist but he wasn't. He'd been a heavy weight prizefighter in his youth travelling the fairs and boxing booths of the country and he had the neck of a bull to prove it. I once asked him to show me how to box. He tucked his right hand under his chin and stretched out his left hand as far as it would go. The Marquis of Queensberry would have been proud. But not of his attitude to War. He just had no argument with the Germans and despised the politicians who had. So he wouldn't go and was punished for it.

Mother told me the story of how one winter's day the warders at the Scrubs asked him if he'd like a bath. He said that he would and he was marched outside into the exercise yard. He was stripped naked in front of the assembled inmates and told to get into a tin bath filled with icy water, which had been put there.

He was later moved to the Glass House at Colchester barracks but no stories of life there survived him.

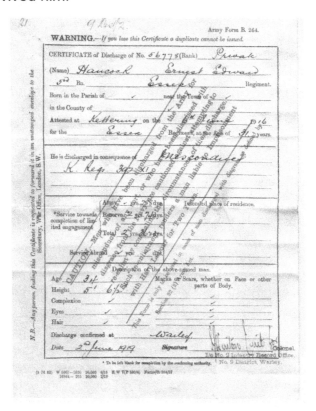

My mother was born in January 1915 but he was not imprisoned until shortly before War was ended.

Here is a copy of his certificate of discharge dated 2nd June 1919. The grounds were 'misconduct.' He had been in the Army reserve for 2 years 74 days, and imprisoned for 288 days.

I'm sure my Grandad was aware of the irony of the red printed warning against attempting to re-enlist!

After the War he resumed his business as a Pawnbroker and Gents outfitter. My Mother would have started her senior school 11 years later but the War had not been forgotten and according to her she was 'sent to Coventry' by the girls at her school. There were only two girls that ever spoke to her or were allowed by their parents to speak to her, the daughter of a consci. The two girls later became my godmothers. My 'Aunt' Laura and my 'Aunt' Nancy who lived in Corby.

Aunt Nancy was a remarkable person. As a young woman she decided she wanted to go to China. On her own. This involved long journeys by boat, rail and road. That was remarkable enough, but she decided when she was there that she wanted to bring back with her a willow pattern dinner service. Easier than it sounds as it was in a box that she couldn't even lift. But she did somehow get it back, persuading fellow travelers, railway porters and sailors to lift the box for her. I'm not sure if she appreciated that she could have bought a willow pattern dinner service at any Department store in the Country. China was a long way to go! But then again what else would you bring back from China apart from...china! In her flat in Corby she had the plates displayed on a china shelf. Ironic!

She never married. Another whose potential husband was killed in the War. She was a schoolteacher all her life and was eventually appointed Head teacher to the Village School in Stoke Albany. Yes, she was an eccentric and behaved very strangely. But as the world became more cautious of strange people she was eventually forced by the parents to not only resign from her post, but she was put into a 'home'. My Mother went to visit her but felt her manner was no different to when she was younger. It was people's perceptions that had changed. Mother was pretty upset about this.

Your knowledge of your Grandparents is usually confined to what your parents tell you about them and maybe there's another filtering system, you only remember the things that stick in your mind and why do they stick in your mind? With me the things I remember are the things that made my Mother angry.

There must have been things she remembered which were good. Which made her smile and maybe there was but my Mother's anger was so frightening to me growing up that the things that made her angry were the things that stuck in my consciousness. Without realizing it, family life as I was growing up consisted of trying to keep Mother happy. There was no room for anyone else's feelings or needs. Her moods dominated which is how she controlled the world around her. The effect on me, though I didn't know it, was devastating. My entire energy was concentrated on making my Mother happy. I was trying to be the parent to her child. My 'child' had no parent. My Father was too busy tiptoeing around Mother's moods!

My Mother was taught to drive a car by her Father when she was 16. There were no age limits and no driving tests in those days. She had her photo in the local paper for being the first girl to drive herself to school. Sadly no copy of this was kept.

She spoke French fairly fluently thanks to a pen friend she had who lived in Paris. She stayed with her in Paris for some time but only after her Father had driven her there in his Austin 7 to make sure the family were suitable and that she would be safe.

She passed the School Certificate which in her day was like passing 12 GCSEs with starred 'A's. Or so she told me. She could have gone to train as a nurse but my Grandfather thought that nursing in those days was for glorified cleaning maids. So she went to St Peter's teacher training college in Peterborough. The Principal was a lady who was one of the group of children who had Alice in Wonderland read to them in Oxford, by the Author Lewis Carroll, as he was writing them.

My Mother learned a lot about trees during her time at College but I wish she had leaned more about bringing up children.

She was quite good with children under the age of 8 but had great difficulty relating to anyone older. If you didn't mind being treated like you were 8 she was fine. If you didn't mind her being an authority about everything that was fine. If you didn't mind her finishing your sentences that was fine too. She always could because she always knew what you were thinking. She never needed to ask so she never did. Except she could never have imagined what I was thinking and if she did and she ignored it then she really was an evil person. And I don't think she was.

I don't know whether being a pawnbroker carried any additional stigma. If people hated you because your Dad was a consci I don't suppose it mattered that he was a pawnbroker as well. She often told the story of how my Father's Mother asked my Grandad what he did for a living when they first met although she knew very well. She wanted to hear him say he was a pawnbroker just to humiliate him. His neck was so strong he could never wear a tie. That always made him look a bit disheveled.

An article appeared in the local newspaper about his business. It says that he would even take pledges on horses. 'When the Army was in Rockingham Road Park in the First World War any of their horses that weren't up to standard were sold. The gypsies used to buy them and bring them to me.' He would allow £30 on a horse but insist on fodder being provided for it. 'They would always collect them again. They never left them for many days.' On Saturday nights, women used to bring in their husbands newly washed shirts and underclothes. They were wet so they were hung up to dry ready for work on Monday morning.' There were many tragic cases, the Article continues, the woman who had a baby on Friday and was pledging the baby clothes on the Saturday, and the woman who walked 11 miles from Market

Harborough to raise £1 to keep the bailiff from her door.'
As you will see from this newspaper article he was a very brave man. The attack he suffered finished him off mentally and physically and he never recovered. It was such a shame.

My Mother was often asked to give a talk about pawnbroking to Women's Institutes and the like and she always ended with the Pawnbrokers Prayer.

A pawnbroker stood at the Golden Gate
His head was bent and low.
He meekly asked the Man of Fate
The way that he should go.

'What have you done,' St Peter asked,
'To gain admission here?'

I kept a Pawnbroker's shop down below
For many and many a year.

St Peter opened wide the gate
And gently pushed the bell.
'Come inside and choose your harp,
You've had your share of hell.'

It's a fitting tribute to a man who had suffered so much and only tried to be kind to whoever needed his kindness.

When I was at my infant's school one day Mrs. Palmer, my teacher, was talking to the class about the various signs that used to hang outside shops, used in an era where few adults could read. She asked if anyone knew the sign for a pawnbroker, only 'Steve' wasn't allowed to answer. There was silence, nobody knew. 'Steve, tell the class.' I was mortified I was supposed to know but didn't. There was what seemed to be a huge silence. I felt terrible. Mrs. Palmer told the class it was three gold balls. I had no idea because my Grandad didn't have the usual sign to spare his customers the shame. Poverty was shameful. The three balls were part of the Coat of Arms of the Medici Family and represent the three purses of gold given to three virgins by St Nicholas of Bari, the same St Nicholas of Santa Claus fame, to enable them to marry. It later represented the two to one chance against the pledge being redeemed.

My Father won thefootball pools as a young man and decided to take himself off to Hamburg to stay with a pen friend, Detliff Waechter. By all accounts he had a pretty good time! Detliff's Father was Professor of English at Hamburg University. He wrote a textbook, which was to become a standard work on English Idioms. He was writing it whilst my Father was staying with the family and would often come down from his study and ask him what the idiom was for a particular phrase or saying. An example was the saying for going for a night on the town. My Father told him the expression was 'going on the razzle.' This and a lot of other 1930's slang was dutifully entered into the book which was then learned by a generation of German students. I still have a copy of the book.

He returned from Germany with just enough money for the bus fare from Leicester station! The pools win all spent!

My Father, as a result of his time in Hamburg spoke fluent German and had many German friends. My Mother mentioned that shortly before War broke out they were visited by various young German men who all wanted to be taken to the South Coast. They were happy to oblige!

I once asked my Mother to write down her life story. After she died I found what she had written. This is the passage that deals with how she met my Father, "Jan 6th 1939, I went into Leicester to go to Alderman Newton's Girls School for St John Ambulance. First Aid Certificate. I was living at 32 Vicarage Lane Humberstone teaching at Humberstone School. Had a bad cold. Went into a Milk Bar for a Milk Shake. Wanted a black Currant one but they didn't have any. Someone followed me out and when I was looking in a shoe shop, whoever it was said, 'this is your hankey, you dropped it in the Milk Bar.' I said, 'thank you,' and walked on. But the young man still followed me and eventually spoke to me again and asked if he could walk with me. We looked in Broughton and Jones' window. Eventually Richard walked me down Churchgate to where I was going, Philharmonic Choir Practice and arranged to meet him outside Lee's Clock on Thursday. We did, and went to the Odeon Cinema and saw 'Sixty Glorious Years.' January 30th came (her birthday) and we went to a dance at The Palais. Then on March 1st I cycled to Broughton and Jones and Richard gave me my engagement ring. I got another bad cold after Easter and it developed into Pneumonia. Had to have test for TB but it was OK. Richard and I went to Bournemouth for a week. We eventually decided to buy 17 Marydene Drive. Had to wait until December 2nd to move in, difficulty getting materials to finish due to War. We were married September 21st 2.30 p.m. On the run up to our wedding, first one couldn't come, called up for War service. Fear of bombs etc so numbers were depleted. Uncle Jack at Uffcombe (Devon) made my three tier wedding cake. I had to fetch it from the railway station on the morning of my wedding."

I wonder how many would tell the story of meeting their future Partner of fifty years marriage without expressing one single word of emotion, or even describing what he looked like, what sort of person he was. Quite extraordinary.

The Headmistress at Humberstone School was a Miss Attenborough, the Aunt of the famous Attenborough brothers David and Richard. My Uncle Robert was in the same class at school as Richard Attenborough and described him as a 'cry baby.' He did well enough though!

By the time war broke out in 1939 my Mother and Father had married. My Mother was an Infants teacher. My Father worked in his Father's Ironmongers shop. When it came for my Father to be called up something mysterious happened. A fit young man of 2 and a County cricketer, he was somehow declared unfit for active service and drafted into a munitions factory. This didn't go down too well with people in the area who not only 'sent them to Coventry' for the entire duration of the War and for years afterwards but also posted seven white feathers through the letterbox. The badge of cowardice. Curiously my Mother told me this but never told my Father. Even when my brother was born in 1945 the neighbours stayed away.

He bragged that he wasn't very good at factory work and was put into the stores, his main job being to ensure that the stock matched the Inventory. If he had too much stock he would bring the surplus home with him to balance the books. We had a small orchard with a concrete path round it. It's still there and little do the current owners know that beneath the path lie dozens of Spitfire parts. This was his contribution to the war effort!

Mother told the story about how her Father was able to get petrol rations on the basis that he had to transport Aunt Flo, a cripple, to Leicester for 'treatment.' One day he took her on a trip from Kettering to Leicester to see my Mother.

The neighbours tipped off the Police who came knocking at the door. He explained that he was allowed to take his wife's Sister on outings, she being a cripple. He was required to produce the alleged Aunt. Being so tiny she couldn't be seen in the car. Grandad called to Flo that there was a 'gentleman' wanting to meet her and she appeared at the door to the embarrassment of the policeman who promptly closed his notebook and left. You can see a picture of the family against the world and the family victorious.

My Father was appointed an Air Raid Warden. He was supposed to keep watch from a shelter in the village but only did this once. He spent the rest of the War being a Warden from the comfort of his bedroom! They often spoke of the bombing in Coventry. They could see the flames from the bottom of the garden. There was no expression of regret at the loss of life just a simple wonder at how far away they were and still able to see the flames. Leicester was only bombed once and that was by a plane that should have been bombing Coventry but got lost on the way there. Near my village was another village called Stoughton where there was a now disused wartime aerodrome. From here the gliders that took men to the landing at Arnhem in Holland took off on their ill-fated invasion of Europe. It was a good place to cycle to as you could find spent bullet cartridge cases at the old firing range.

I was, of course, the son of a coward and wondered later in life whether the neighbours stopped their children from being friends with me because of it. Other boys were forever playing in our garden but I never ventured into theirs.

Have a good look at these photos. Two of them were taken by my Father. He had a wonderful way of taking photos cutting off all the heads! Brilliant. The one in the middle with the heads on was taken by my Mother.

My Dad's Father, William Broughton, is on the far left next to my Granny Broughton, Daisy. Then my Father, Big Dick, then my Uncle Bob, then my beloved Grandad Hancock. The only man not wearing a collar and therefore to be despised and rejected by Broughtons one and all. In reality his neck was so thick and strong no collar would ever fit comfortably. He is also the only man smiling which says a lot. Next to him, Nanna Hancock and next to her mad Aunt Nancy. Holding baby dick is my Aunt Laura, my other Godmother. She also never married and spent her life working in the Smedley's pea factory in Kings Lynn Norfolk. I must hasten to add she was a secretary not a factory girl! The little boy on the left is the odious Marcus, the eldest Broughton Grandchild, perceptibly taller than my brother on the right, keeping well away from him to avoid comparisons! All will be explained shortly!

My Broughton Grandparents never visited us again. They didn't like us much. They only visited the house once more after the christening even though they only lived a mile away and that was when they knew we were on holiday. Whenever we went on holiday after that we had to tidy the house and close all the curtains just in case they came 'snooping.' My Father visited his parents on the way home from work but that was it. I think they didn't approve of my Mother. We were very occasionally taken to their house to be 'measured'. This involved being taken to the pantry and a carving knife placed on our heads to mark the point we had reached.

My Brother, who was older than me, always had his height greeted with the statement, 'not as tall as Marcus.' Marcus was the eldest grandchild and always likely to be taller! Nothing we ever did was as good as Marcus. It was very satisfying that Marcus failed his 11 plus and spent his entire working career compiling the Telephone Directory. I suppose someone had to do it in the days before computers. He also never married and never left home! He later changed his name to John. It was to become a family tradition. My Father was very scathing about this. Why should anyone want to change their name? I should, to do my cousins justice, mention Marcus's sister who distinguished herself by appearing on Countdown. She was quite a family celebrity!

On one occasion and one occasion only, we were taken into My Grandparents sitting room to be shown to my Grandfather. He didn't say any thing and we were promptly shown out again. I have no way of knowing whether this was normal for the post-Edwardian era or not. I grew up being told that 'little boys should be seen but not heard' and this experience seemed to reinforce in my mind that this was true!

I have a cousin whose branch of the family has a story about, 'the time Uncle Will spoke.' Only the once mind you. He was carving the turkey one

Christmas and uttered the memorable words, 'cuts like butter!' Only with his Leicester accent it sounded like, 'coots like bootter!' A lifetime and that's all anyone remembers about you!

I was given the name Richard after my Father but when I was about 2 years old my Mother got fed up of my Grandmother referring to my Father as 'big dick' and to me being referred to as 'little dick.' So she decided that I would be called Steve. I suppose I have to be grateful about that although it shows the war that was going on between my Mother and my Father's Mother.

On the wall of the sitting room of the family home were two pictures, one of me and one of my brother. The one of me was taken at about the age of two and bore the name 'Richard'. A constant reminder of the child that was never allowed to be himself. The child that had to be changed to suit his Mother's fancy. The child that withered and died. She took away my name and with that my identity. I began a lifetime trying to be what my Mother wanted, trying to please her, never succeeding and little by little the person I would have been, Richard, died.

I only learned whilst writing this that my Mother and Grandmother shared the same birthday. Funny that this was never ever mentioned. Funny that we never celebrated Granny's birthday.

It was also never mentioned in the family that my Father had an Uncle Tom who committed suicide in 1919. I imagined he was another consci, but he wasn't. .As a witness at the Inquest was reported in the local paper as saying, 'the deceased died in a cow shed on his farm, a gun by his side. He complained of flatulence and indigestion which kept him awake at night, but never said he would take his own life. He was worried about his heart but it was alright.' His widow said he was depressed at times but he had no financial or family troubles. He had said, 'you need not worry I shall not take my own life.' The report ends, 'the witness had the impression that the deceased was neurotic.' I think that must have been a fair assumption!

He had another Uncle, Harry, who I met on only one occasion. He had been gassed in the trenches and was always an invalid with a bad chest. The Great War left its mark on the 5.5 million soldiers who took part and on those left behind at home.

My Mother had an Uncle Arthur who was shelled in the trenches. Part of his skull was blown away and he was given a steel plate to replace it. Uncle Arthur suffered the most colossal headaches and only my Mother with her 'healing hands' could ease the pain. He was a hairdresser and ran a salon in Kettering where, after the War, he introduced the 'permanent wave' to the ladies of Nothamptonshire. It was a tremendous success and in time he ran a whole chain of 'Greenaways' Salons. Greenaway was his name and not a reference to the effect of his hairdressing. If it had been then I suppose the salons would have been called 'Greyaways' but they weren't!

In the 1960's he committed suicide by drowning in the boating lake at Wickstead Park in Kettering. Quite an achievement as the boating lake was only about 6 inches deep. My Mother always claimed it was an accident because he had a return bus ticket in his pocket when he died. Maybe though it was one of those spur of the moment things but maybe it wasn't.

My brother was born in 1945 and in our village at the time was a Prisoner of War Camp. Not at all like the German camps I read about in my Father's collection of wartime adventure storybooks. Here the prisoners were free to go back to Germany but didn't want to. Their homes were in the Russian occupied part of Germany and they were better off in the Camp. To pass the time they were encouraged to help out with families in the village who needed help in the garden. A man called Richard Schmidt worked for my parents but took more interest in the new baby than in the garden. My Mother decided that she would rather look after the garden than the baby so my brother was cared for by this kindly member of Hitler's notorious Storm Troopers. I can imagine what the neighbours thought! We now had Big Dick and Herr Richard with little dick coming along later!

When I was 3 my brother was 6 and he joined the church choir. This was fairly normal in villages in those days. The church was still at the centre of village life apart from the non-conformists for whom the chapel was at the centre of village life. There were 3 places in our village, which were sinister places that I used to cross the road to avoid if possible. The chapel was one. 'They don't kneel down to pray and they don't have bishops' as my Mother would often say. This seemed terribly wicked indeed to me. In old age she succumbed and went to a funeral of a friend at the Chapel. 'It was perishing,' she said, adding thereby another accusation to the list of things to condemn the Chapel!

One Christmas I was due to go to the Church Christmas party but turned up on the wrong day so attended the Chapel Christmas party. It was so terrible an experience that to this day I get very nervous before attending social occasions and do anything I can to avoid them!

The next place to avoid at all costs was the Co-op. This was also a shameful place but I was never told why. I think it was because poor people went there. All I knew about the Co-op was that people went for the 'divi' which was apparently a terribly shameful thing.

The third place was the Cedars public house. Drink was a very wicked thing and I only had to think of what happened to Aunt Flo to know where it led. There was a lady in our road who was an alcoholic. She used to cycle to the Cedars at lunchtime wearing sunglasses. She only just managed the return journey!

It was unheard of for women to go to pubs let alone on their own and on bicycles. I used to imagine

Jesus being in our village, standing outside the Cedars preaching about the evils of drink!

So, when my brother joined the choir, I wanted to go too. According to my Mother, she told me I had to wait until I could read so I set about teaching myself to read with my brother's help. About 6 months later I could read well enough to sing a hymn or two so I was allowed to join. I remember being so small I couldn't see over the pew so I had to balance on two hassocks. I do remember being desperate to start school as well, and being in a village I was allowed to go about a year before I was old enough to be put on the register.

Mrs. Palmer was our teacher and I remember my first day. I was given some
wooden letters to trace round.

I loved the choir and I loved going to school. I wonder if they were both places I could escape from my Mother's moods? Going to Church twice a week for choir practice, twice on Sundays and sometimes twice on Saturdays for weddings, I was immersed in bible stories. I nearly used the word 'submersed' and that may have been more accurate. I knew I had to be good to have any chance of making my Mother happy but I now learned that I had to be like Jesus. It was a hard act to follow, especially if no one approved of you the way you were or even noticed you. So I learned that humility was the key. Pride was a terrible sin and the world's greatest criminals were the Pharisees and the Sadducees. Like Jesus I ended up being crucified so let that be a lesson to you!

And the person that was me disappeared in the process. And I knew that however hard I tried I couldn't for a moment think I was OK because that was pride rearing its evil head. And for sure no one ever said I was OK. My Mother had this rule that she should treat me and my brother the same. So when I passed the 11 plus and my brother didn't, my success was ignored because it might have made my Brother resentful. It was always very painful to me that nothing I could do could be recognized because it would make my brother resentful. It wouldn't, because he just wasn't and isn't the resentful type! My

Mother could only see the world as it affected her. She had no way of imagining how anyone else might feel, least of all her children.

My escape from my Mother's moods came with the choir and with school. It also came in expeditions with my small band of friends 'down the fields'. We would be Robin Hood, with or without Richard Green. We would be the Lone Ranger and Tonto. Hawkeye and the Last of the Mohicans, Lancelot and all those programmes which fired our imagination. We were the second family in our road to have a TV. So there! The people with the first had an electrical shop, which was, like cheating and therefore didn't count! I can remember sitting cross-legged on the floor, eyes glued to 'the box,' being told off for getting too close. It was thought that a kind of radiation came from tellys and sitting too close was bad for you. I even used to watch the 'Test' card. When there was no program on, the BBC used to show a card so that repair men had something to go by. They always played music with it and I just loved listening to it. Simple pleasures!

I can remember the day when I felt my childhood had ended. I was reading a magazine and saw an advert for a cowboy outfit, 'suit ages 5 to 7.' It was just what I had always wanted. I was 7, but nearly 8, and I thought that I was now too old to have a cowboy outfit and I never ever would. The feeling of sadness and disappointment I had lives with me today. Maybe it was just not being able to have the cowboy outfit!

Later as I got older I would venture further afield on my bike spending many hours by the side of a canal with my fishing rod. I never caught very much but I did love the stillness, the water, the creatures that lived alongside the water's edge. I was fascinated by the ripples in the water. How you could throw in a stone and the ripples continued long after the stone had disappeared. War had its effect like that as did parenting and so many human endeavors. And how painful the journey back to that stone and its thrower. And the reason why.

I ultimately had the choir taken away from me. There was always a Head boy and when it was time for me to become Head boy, having been there the longest, another boy, Stuart Edwards was chosen. I was desolate feeling total rejection. My Mother persuaded me to join her Church as an altar server, they didn't have a choir, so I lost my church and my singing the centre of my life.

Here I am, the angelic choirboy....the one in the front....the tubby one looking at the hymn book. Well lots of people thought I was angelic and wrote to the newspaper about it. Stuart Edwards is the odious looking boy to the left. On the right is Roger Wheatley. Like me he passed the 11 plus and went to Wyggeston. Unlike me he was given a bike as a present for doing so!

Part of finding Little Dick came with joining a choir, which I did in later life after a gap of about 30 years or more. I love singing and the harmonies you make. I have now sung many times at The Albert Hall in London. It was always a huge thrill and I'm quite glad my Mother never lived to see that and spoil it for me. She would have bragged about it to her friends, which I would have hated. My greatest singing moment came on September 11th 2011 singing 'the Armed Man' at the Lincoln Centre in New York conducted by the composer Karl Jenkins. Quite a thrill, but again nobody there to say, 'well done.'

My Father's escape was the garden. He worked in the family shop 6 days a week and spent all of Sunday in the garden. Apart from, that is, about an hour on a Sunday afternoon when both parents went to bed and my brother and I had to amuse ourselves.

Father was keen that we should be good cricketers. We were sent to a cricket 'school' one evening a week. I have to say that we were both useless. He even erected a cricket net in the garden with a sisal mat to ensure a perfect surface. He would place coins on the ground where the ball had to bounce. If you hit a coin you could keep it. We didn't make much from this game. It was as if he would only take an interest if we shared his talent for cricket. We didn't and he lost interest in us both.

He had the annoying habit of addressing me through a third party, hence, 'what's he doing Mother?' It was like we didn't exist.

My brother was hard of hearing. Not deaf because he could hear quite well really apart from the beginnings and ends of words. But he was an instinctive lip reader. So while I laid in bed listening to my parents arguing and arguing. He was oblivious to it all and lay sleeping. There are many families with a handicapped child. In these families the non handicapped child often suffers from not having the attention that child needed. In many families it is inevitable as hard pressed parents do there best. In my family it was a deliberate policy!

My isolation was total. Locked in a world controlled by my Mother's moods. Powerless to make her happy. Totally dependent for my own happiness on her being happy and try as I might I never achieved that. It made me feel responsible for my own unhappiness. I had to be reminded that in that relationship, she was the parent and I was the child. I thought I was at fault, inadequate but that's how you end up. It's very wrong and very sad and many young people share that experience.

I felt totally responsible for making her happy. My Fathers words so often spoken, still ring in my ears, 'be nice to your Mother, Steve, she's in a mood.' 'You know what she's like.' And he escaped into the garden. It just made my brother angry which is what it should have done to me. Maybe it did but there was nobody to hear my anger and distress so I learned to put up with it. I learned never to express it. I learned that if I did it would just make things worse. Like the babies that stop crying when nobody picks them up. I stopped having feelings except the feeling of wishing I was dead. No, that's wrong. I did have feelings. I just couldn't express them, and was afraid to. Still am.

The greatest most crushing tragedy came when I developed acne. Most boys do and mine wasn't as bad as most. If I could have worn a bucket over my head I would have done. I suffered total agony. Humiliated, embarrassed, ashamed. I had some cream I put on to try to hide them but it never worked. I would do my best, think I'd succeeded, venture down stairs to be greeted with, 'that's an angry spot you've got.' I could have murdered her. It was said in an arrogant, almost triumphant way. 'Aha, gotcha, that'll hurt you,' and it gave her total victory, total control. She had me just where she wanted me.

As a result I confined myself to my bedroom. Desperate to go to University or anywhere so I could get away. Which is just what I did.

CHAPTER 2 THE KITCHEN

The kitchen is the stage on which the drama of domestic life is played. The family are the actors on the stage. In the play, which formed my childhood, the principal role was played by my Mother. She was the star of the show and around her the drama unfolded. I was trying hard to be like Jesus which somehow made her the Virgin Mary or Gladys as she was known in her youth. We were players with lesser parts. Big Dick, my Father, me, little dick and my brother Eddie. The script was written for us by the generations that went before. How many of us played ourselves?

The stage was small and typical of the 1950's. Stage right was the kitchen sink. Stainless steel (most people had white enamel, we were pretty upmarket) and with a window overlooking the garden where my Mother could keep an eye on my Father's gardening exploits. The window would fly open, 'No Richard, that's not a weed, that's a plant.' She wasn't joking either. Stage left, was the door to the hall and next to it a Frigidaire fridge. An early model with a freezing compartment just big enough for a block of Walls' ice cream or one pack of Birdseye frozen peas. Frozen peas were later replaced by a new invention, 'Surprise' peas which were the first freeze dried vegetable and quite surprising as their name suggested.

On the fridge was the radio. Before transistors were invented radios were large things with valves that had to heat up before the sound came out. There were only three stations, the Light Wave, the Home

Service and the Third Programme which no one listened to because of its' boring highbrow music. The dial on the radio listed hundreds of continental stations none of which you could hear however carefully you turned the dial. On the radio we listened to programmes like, 'The Billy Cotton Band Show,' 'wakey wakey,' shouted Billy quite regularly, 'The Navy Lark,' with John Pertwee, and 'Workers Playtime' where they visited factories, played games and gave away small amounts of money held by 'Mable at the Table' compered by the wonderful Wilfred Pickles.

Every afternoon was 'Women's Hour', which I loved because it was so interesting. I also listened to 'The Archers' and 'Mrs. Dale's Diary' but then everybody did. The high spot on Sundays was 'Two Way Family Favourites' where people 'at home' sent messages to loved ones in the forces overseas and vice versa. In the days before long distance telephones hearing these messages exchanged was positively gripping. There was no television except in the early evening so we would sit round the table in the kitchen listening especially when the weather was bad.

At the back of the kitchen was not surprisingly the back door. To the left was the pantry. Nobody has a pantry now but in those days it was vital. Here was stored all the bottled and pickled garden produce which kept us going through the winter. Everybody used 'Kilner Jars,' which had a rubber sealing ring. No home could exist without them. There was one weekend in about September when our shop would sell nothing but Kilner Jars and rings to go with them and now we buy fresh produce flown to the supermarkets from all over the world.

My Grandfather's hobby was shooting innocent pheasants, hares and partridges, which were left to hang in the pantry thereby enhancing the flavour. My brother was terrified of the dead birds and avoided going into the pantry at all costs. On the floor of the pantry were large brown bottles of various beverages including beer and cider. If you returned the bottles to the shop you'd be given 2d each. This was true recycling. I owe my life to a bottle of cider. As a toddler I was very ill with gastric flu and couldn't keep anything down. The Doctor had run out of ideas and I was becoming dangerously ill. I toddled into the pantry and asked my Mother for a glass of cider. It made me rather 'wobbly' and I fell over the dog and asked to go to bed. When I woke up I was cured. It was a miracle! I've always been partial to a glass of cider, which always has a similar wobbling effect!

The back door was the main entrance for lesser players in the drama that was everyday life. The baker came with a selection of bread and cakes in a wicker basket. 'What are we having today Mrs Broughton?' Our main meal was 'tea' which you ate with jam and bread, just like the song in 'The Sound of Music' so the bread man was essential to life! The fishmonger came, as well as the milkman and the grocer known conveniently for a weekly visitor as Mr. Weekes. Mother phoned in the order, which was delivered a few days later. It predated Internet shopping by about 50 years and was much more friendly. You will find this hard to believe but once a year a man came from Belgium delivering strings of onions on a bike. I must be one of the few people left in the world who can string onions in the traditional way. It may be useful one day! We became friends with him and often visited his farm in Belgium where the onions were grown. Women at home with children had much less isolation in those days with all these tradesmen popping in and out. And they were all men. There were very few jobs for women except in the factories hospitals and schools.

I can even remember a man coming on a bicycle to sharpen knives. His bike somehow converted to power a grindstone where the knives were expertly placed to be sharpened. I know this play is becoming like a scene from Mary Poppins but that's how it was! And yes, we also had to have a chimney sweep
who used rods with a bristle brush on the end.

Once a year a blind gentleman came to tune Mother's piano. There were no guide dogs in those days but somehow he managed to find his way unfailingly to the house. You can learn a lot about music from a piano tuner!

This was a world in stark contrast to the world where Mothers now bring up their children There was none of the isolation which characterises modern life. Mothers didn't have to combine childcare with work and domestic life which was full of visitors to the kitchen, trades people and the like. You hardly ever hear now of a television needing repair but the TV repairman was a regular visitor to most homes lucky enough to have a TV. Children had almost total freedom to wander where and how they liked. I was aware of not taking lifts in cars with strangers so stranger danger was clearly something that parents worried about even then. Depression was unheard of despite the low standard of living. Maybe there's a lesson here.

Through the back door was a passage with the coal hole and an 'outside' toilet with a high flush. Very cold in winter but one step ahead of my Nanna's 'outside' toilet which really was 'outside.' For some reason I was always frightened by the sound of the toilet flushing and would try to get out as quickly as possible. The house was dependent on coal. The coal men were also frequent visitors but never made it to the kitchen. The kitchen housed the Raeburn, which was coal fired. The Raeburn provided hot water, an oven and two hotplates. It also made a good place to sit and warm your backside to cries of, 'you'll get piles,' but as I didn't know what piles might be it wasn't much of a threat.

The only other source of heat in the entire house was a coal fire in the living room. This usually sent smoke into the room if the wind was in the wrong direction. There was a constant battle to stop it smoking. Different chimney pots, different grates in the hearth and eventually an enclosed stove type contraption. In the worst weather my Dad brought out a series of paraffin heaters which made the whole house damp and warm at the same time which was better than cold and dry! The smell of the paraffin was wonderful if you liked that sort of thing. By 'warm' I mean just above freezing. Even with paraffin heaters the windows had ice on the insides, your flannel was frozen in the bathroom and the water in the toilet cistern frequently froze.

So, the stage was set.

Act 1. Scene 1. Sunday lunch. This was a great event and began with a trip down the garden with a spade to dig the 'taters'. My Mother delegated most of the work as she hated housework. Other family members would wash and peel the taters and whatever vegetable was in season. Meat was hanging in the pantry and had to be skinned and disembowelled. When I tried to prepare a chicken 40 years later I found I could still pluck and draw like a professional. One of the hazards of eating meat in my family was the lead shot that you found in nearly every bite. Not in the chickens though. Even Grampa Broughton didn't shoot chickens. He hated pigeons though and was reputed to keep a shotgun under his bed to shoot them from the bedroom window. This was quite a surprise to Granny who was often still asleep when the shooting commenced! The family is, however strangely proud of his achievement in shooting two rare flying geese. Two shots from two barrels. They had to hit in the eyes because the birds' feathers were too thick to be penetrated at distance by the lead shot. They were so rare one was stuffed and is still on display in Leicester museum. What happened to the other? The family ate it!

I had a healthy appetite and ate most things, not that there was much variety. No pasta in those days. Mainly meat and two vedge. My brother hated cheese so we never had cheese. There were only two things I couldn't stomach. Apple pie and brussel sprouts. My Mother's apple pie was particularly nasty but sprouts! Just couldn't do it. I was locked in the pantry and not allowed out till I'd eaten them. I spent many Sunday afternoons in the pantry! I remember looking one day at the contents of the shelf that was low enough for me to see. There was a tin, a very small tin, of Nescafe coffee. It was only opened once and then I realised why it was there. It was in case someone came for coffee. No-one ever did apart from one occasion when Mrs. Vaughan came from across the road.

Wartime feuds must have been forgotten temporarily. She came with the news that shocked me to the core. Dinah, her daughter, was a nurse and was involved nursing patients with Polio. There was a terrible epidemic at the time. Later on vaccinations were invented. Polio patients were paralysed and Dinah had done something, unmentionable in front of small boys, to her 'insides' so she wouldn't be able to have children. It was caused by all the lifting of Polio victims. To this day I can't bear to see women carry anything bigger than a handbag. In supermarkets I offer to help complete strangers of childbearing age with their shopping. They don't usually appreciate the offer so I have lately stopped offering. Dinah eventually married and I embroidered (I quite liked embroidery!) a set of napkins with a matching tablecloth as a wedding present. We weren't invited. The Vaughans were 'posh' and their boys went to Private School at Uppingham. The Father had a furniture factory. Embroidery was quite a hobby, which I learned when I had my appendix out. Recovery was slower in those days so it gave me something to do.

Act 1. Scene 2. Gallstones. My Mother once collapsed in the kitchen in terrible agony. It was gallstones and she was carted off to hospital to have them taken away. We had to look after ourselves whilst she was away but that was OK. Her cooking was so bad it was a relief to cook for ourselves. I was the only person I knew who actually preferred to have school dinners! On another occasion she collapsed after being stung by a wasp. I phoned the Doctor but the receptionist told me to make her a cup of tea. She was unconscious so that wasn't much help. I then phoned an ambulance and I suppose saved her life. Nobody mentioned it though. I was 7 years old and had never used the phone before. I think I did quite well. I shall never forget our number 36635. Funny that, how some numbers stick with you.

Act 1. Scene 3. Hot fat. Etched into my memory is the time when my Mother took out of the oven a bowl of hot fat. She put it down on the floor because it was too hot to hold with the cloth she had. I had no shoes on, didn't see the bowl of fat and promptly put my foot in it. I was off school for weeks and had to have penicillin poultices to stop infection. I still remember the pain.

Act.2. Scene 1. Formica. The day this new invention came to the kitchen was a great day! The kitchen table was wooden and was always getting damaged, stained, marked and generally looked rough. Now an occasional visitor to the house was Mr. James our painter and decorator. Mr. James drove a Morris 1000 pickup van in a 'strange for the time' orange colour. He had a handlebar moustache and must have been in the RAF during the War. Well he looked as if he had. On one of his visits Mr. James suggested covering the table with this new wonder substance. Formica! It changed like in the kitchen. You could glue models, paint them, do simple carpentry all without fear of damaging the table. Formica was to tables what lederhosen was to boys bottoms! I loved Mr. James. He introduced us to wood chip wallpaper, which saved us from patterned paper, which was all you could have before that. He also put my train set on a board on pulleys above my Brother's bed so it could be put out of the way when not in use. What a wonderful man!

Act 2. Scene 2. Laundry. To the right of the back door was the washing machine. It was a mighty beast bearing the name, 'Thor'. In the days before front loaders it was a top loader and much more advanced than the more common 'twin tub' where you had to take your washing from the washing tub to the drying tub, usually with wooden tongs. There was nothing 'automatic' about the 'Thor'. It had a lever at the front to change functions but it was a great washing machine. When it went onto its spin programme the house shook with the ferocious power of it. Thor was well named after the god of War!

Mother hated ironing, nothing unusual there, but she somehow mastered the art of ironing with a rotary iron, even shirts, and boasted that she cut ironing time to a fraction. In her later years she often did her ironing in the middle of the night as she couldn't sleep and had nothing else to do! Hanging from the ceiling was a railing device, sometimes called a lazy daisy, where wet washing was hung to dry in the winter. In the days before tumble dryers and radiators, it was a great invention you winched up and down with a cord. The invention of the drip-dry shirt known as the Rael Brook Poplin was a great boon as it did away with ironing although it was particularly nasty for men to wear!

Act 2. Scene 3. The visit. Occasionally we had a visit from Nanna and Grandad, usually on a Sunday when the shop was shut. They would bring a penguin biscuit with them. This was a great treat but nothing compared with the day Grandad arrived with a basket full of conkers. He'd stopped on the way and collected them for me. I was completely overwhelmed by this kindness. I kept that basket of conkers for many years and as they hardened they stood me in good stead for playground conker fights. Because it came from someone I really looked up to, that act of kindness meant so much more to me. They always stayed in the kitchen when they came. I suppose that's what family did.

Act 2. Scene 4. The inspiration. My parents decided to put the house on the market and I was trying to study for my 0-levels. One day a family came to look round and they eventually decided to buy it. They had with them a little boy who was apparently very struck by the boy he saw in what was going to be his bedroom studying. He apparently told his parents he was going to be like the big boy who he saw that day. As I progressed in life and eventually went to Cambridge he often repeated to his parents the promise he'd made that he was going to be like the boy in the bedroom. He ended up being awarded a scholarship at Balliol College (I think) Oxford. And all down to me inspiring him!

The Final Act. This came when the house was sold and we moved into my Grandparents' bungalow after they died. I was about 16 and never really forgave them for selling the place that had been my home for all those years, my entire life in fact. All those memories, all those familiar places. Playing in the street with my friends, down the fields, digging holes to reach Australia, lighting fires, helping with the harvest, feeding the donkey who lived in the field at the bottom of the garden. All gone. Any chance I had of saving a little bit of little dick was gone.

CHAPTER 2.2 THE BEDROOM

If the kitchen is the stage on which the drama of domestic life is played then the bedroom is the place where the ups and downs of mental health are confronted. It's a place to retreat to; perhaps a place of safety but sometimes a place of danger where you may decide to put an end to your suffering. I often think that depression lurks indoors; the outdoors is less likely to trap and snare you.

I remember once lying on my back in the middle of a field, miles from nowhere, completely on my own and feeling (good word that) that this was the real world. The stress and pressures of life don't exist in the world of sun and sky, they fade into insignificant memories. As a teenager I would cycle miles to be beside a canal and fish. You can sit on the canal bank till darkness comes and be entertained by the busy creatures that inhabit the water's edge. There is constant entertainment, constant pleasure and unbeatable beauty.

Back home the bedroom is an escape from the family but being alone with your thoughts is at times very challenging. Leaving the bedroom to face the outside world can be just the most terrible trial.

Until I was about ten I shared a bedroom with my brother who was three years older than me. He and I were like chalk and cheese. He had a hearing problem and I doubt he ever heard the arguments and rows that went on with our parents downstairs. Whatever makes them think that nobody hears them? He had all that I lacked, self-belief and a capacity to express his feelings, particularly his anger. He also loved reading which I never did and would spend hours with his head buried in a book, G A Henty historical novels were a favourite. His escape was total as he retreated to the world of fiction. I've never seen the point of fiction when you can read about real people but then I've always had this desperate need to work out why I am the way I am and why I'm so unhappy. I need to learn about other people so I can learn about myself. I needed to find little dick.

I had my first slipped disk in my bedroom. I was eleven years old and sitting on the edge of my bed reaching down to put my socks on. When it happens it's like being hit by a bullet or a hammer. BANG. And you're wrecked by the agony that follows. My Mother suffered the same condition, which gave me something else to thank her for! If you're going to have a medical problem there are a lot worse things you can have so I've often contented myself with that thought. It has never stopped me doing what I needed or wanted to do and I usually recovered in three or four days. It also showed me how hopeless the medical profession can be. I once endured the most terrible agony to attend a Doctor's surgery. Bent double I waited for my appointment and dragged my pained frame to his room. He was at his desk and didn't even look up. He started scribbling on his prescription pad. I went through hell to be offered these words of advice, 'go to bed, and here's something if you get constipated, and here's something if you get loose.' That was it. I could have had a thousand other conditions giving that amount of pain but he couldn't be bothered to check.

Duvets hadn't been invented or at least they were a Continental phenomenon, which hadn't yet caught on. Instead we had sheets and blankets and an eiderdown. My Mother prided herself on her 'hospital corners' which was the way nurses tucked in your sheets and blankets. It was quite an art. The most accomplished at it though were the Cambridge bedders. A great amount of time was spent making beds in those days but then married women didn't go out to work, so probably had more time.

I never went to bed without my beloved teddy and kept him until I was about fourteen. I can't remember my brother ever having one though but that was his loss!

The bedroom was where my Mother made her attempt at sex education. I had heard mention of learning about the birds and bees but this just added to the mystery. She sat us down one morning at the foot of my brother's bed and uttered the unforgettable words, 'I can tell by the sheets that you're growing up and I just want to tell you…(there was a long pause)…that if a girl doesn't want to go swimming you mustn't press her. If I was confused before then I was now totally bewildered. But I can honestly say that in all my life I have never pressed a girl to go swimming if she didn't want to. I've been responsible for the existence of four children so the advice was clearly good advice.

With the onset of acne my bedroom became a place of refuge from a world I was desperate to hide from. I never felt bad about going to school as most boys seemed to have the same problem, but I just couldn't bear being in the company of my Mother. Just the thought of her saying, 'that's a nasty spot,' would be too much to bear when I had spent hours trying to hide it with cream. My bedroom became my sanctuary until I could leave and go to University. Strange though it may seem, I doubt I would have got to Cambridge if I hadn't had acne. I had nothing much else to do in my bedroom apart from work.

I began to hate my Mother with a fierce passion. I remember one Christmas Eve seeing her come into our room with our pillowcases. Although I hadn't believed in Father Christmas for many years, it was quite a ritual waking up on Christmas morning and finding our presents at the foot of the bed. I felt disgusted that she couldn't even wait until we were asleep. Disgust was also what I felt at the sight of her in her night-gown. When my brother showed me my first picture of a naked woman in a secret copy of 'Health and Efficiency' it was a middle aged lady standing at the foot of a staircase holding on to the banister rail looking remarkably like my Mother. This too was disgusting. This was the only 'magazine' you could buy but although I tried many times later I was never brave enough to go into a shop and buy it. I bought a lot of comics in those days!

She had this idea that you should open the presents you received in the post before Christmas as they arrived. It meant that you had very little to open on the day itself. People gave much less in those days compared to the huge bonanza that children have now. I remember one Christmas being very excited by the gift of a battery powered speedboat. Nothing large, it was about twelve inches long and I was thrilled to bits, until I discovered there were no batteries. It was very disappointing!

The great invention that transformed bedroom life was the 'Dansette' portable record player. Buying '45's' was to become a great teenage hobby and you would stack them up on the record player spindle to provide about half an hour's entertainment. Pye records had purple labels and were prone to slip when stacked up. They weren't very popular! My favourite recording artist was 'The Shadows' preferably without Cliff Richard and I still have all their records I have a very rare one called 'Saturday Dance' when they were known as 'The Drifters' which I'm very proud of. The bass guitarist of 'The Shadows' was Jet Harris. I was totally smitten and wished I could be him. He had dyed blonde hair and sultry looks. He and Tony Meehan, the drummer, left the Shadows when the others became Jehovah's Witnesses to make records on their own. Tragically Jet was injured in a car crash, turned to alcohol and ended up a few years later as a bankrupt milkman! I saw him on his last tour of the UK and although he was on stage gripping his guitar, he couldn't play a note and had great difficulty standing up. The guitarist in the backing group played all his notes for him! I still thought he was wonderful. He and Tony are now sadly deceased.

Wanting to be Jet Harris I bought (or was given for Christmas) a bass guitar and learned all the music that Jet Harris played. I even formed a band with some friends rehearsing in our garage. It interests me that we would never have had bands with bass guitarists without the pioneering playing of Jet Harris. He was the first musician to import the bass guitar shortly after it was first invented in America. The bands of the Elvis, Buddy Holly era had concert string basses which were plucked and which were generally unsexy!

My record collection consisted almost entirely of instrumentals, which I learned and played along with. Always in my bedroom.

My dressing gown hung on the back of the bedroom door. In the night it looked like a man watching me. Imagination runs amok in your bedroom. Wishing I was dead I hit on the plan that I could simply stop dreaming. I would just slip away quietly and it would all be over. I can now disclose that it doesn't work!

A great salvation for teenagers at the time was the transistor radio, which allowed us to listen to music in our bedrooms or anywhere we wanted. We even had our own radio station, Radio Luxembourg. There were people we came to know as 'disc jockeys' like Jimmy Saville, 'how's about that then?' Even more amazing were 'adverts.' With radio and

TV in the hands of the BBC the world only knew about newspaper and film advertising. This was sensational! There was Horace Batchelor advertising his guaranteed method of winning the football pools. You had to send money to him in Kensham near Bristol which he was always at great pains to spell out, 'that's K E Y N S H A M, Bristol.' Whatever happened to Horace Batchelor, and why didn't the people of Britain win a fortune using his method? Horace Batchelor was probably responsible for an entire generation of teenagers becoming cynical about advertising promises but remarkably good at spelling Keynsham.

After Radio Luxembourg, came the Pirate radio stations, Radio Caroline and the rather more popular Radio London, 'Big L.' Adverts on the Pirate stations became pretty intermittent as the Government tried to stamp them out by making it illegal to advertise with them. Radio London at one time carried just one advert and that was for an Album by 'the Dubliners,' who shared management with the owner of the Station. It was seen as the Government against teenagers and we won! These stations created teenage culture for the first time, which then made the 60's possible. It gave us an identity of our own in post War Britain. War had destroyed the world of our parents and we were establishing new values and a new Society where rules became fewer and standards became a matter of personal choice rather than social convention. When our parents started even more wars in Suez and Vietnam the opposition was massive. 'How dare they take the world to the brink of a World War again? Especially as we were having such fun dancing and listening to the Radio!!'

We were having fun, but we were also creating expectations for ourselves and with those expectations a feeling of frustration and failure for those who felt unable to achieve and compete. Who knows, but I think we were the generation that developed mental illness, particularly depression. People needed a place to go, to retreat from the new culture, the new values of 'if you want it, you can just take it,' so those who couldn't compete could escape from their own unhappiness. The feelings of being fat and being ugly. The feeling of not having all that you perceived others to have. The next generation invented anorexia and self harm which they use as additional escape valves from the pressure cooker of trying to live up to the heights achieved by the beautiful people. Even now I feel the disappointment of not being able to be Jet Harris. Watch 'Pop Idol' and ''The X Factor' and see today's youngsters being publicly devastated by having their dreams shattered. The dreams of my parents' generation were so much easier to achieve. You wanted to get married and have children and that was it. If you were really lucky you had a TV and could afford for a man to come and repair it.

The other day I met a 14-year-old girl who had severe anorexia. She stayed the night. She was involved in a treatment programme and had agreed to have three meals a day of not less than 400 calories. She allowed herself a slice of pizza having seen from the packet how many calories there were. She allowed herself a squirt of tomato ketchup having worked out from the bottle how many calories were in that. And every time she caught sight of herself in the mirror she burst into tears. When I was that age I wouldn't have know what a calorie was. Food didn't come in packets. There were no pizzas. Food was what grew in the garden. Gardens were places that you grew your food. If you didn't have a garden you had to have an allotment. You wouldn't eat otherwise. And people didn't have the chance to get fat and even if they did, nobody minded. What a crap world we've created for her to grow up in. No wonder she doesn't want to be a part of it. I wonder what medication she needs just to survive and how many are there like her?

And then there was yet another great bedroom invention. The tape recorder! What a miracle that was! You could use the little microphone to record music off the radio and listen to it when you wanted to! How about that? You didn't have to buy the record. Thank you God, for technology. It was fab! And if it all got too much you kindly gave us Vallium and the contraceptive pill. What more could you ask? Our happiness and sense of fulfilment was total. And when we thought things couldn't get any better you gave us the Brook Advisory clinic where unmarried couples could get the Pill, just so long as the girls took their boyfriend with them and could persuade the Doctors (female) that they were in stable relationships.

Praise the Lord. Praise Science. Thank God for sex. But where are all the vegetables?

CHAPTER 2.3 THE GARDEN

I find it very curious that there are so many 'experts' now available to design attractive and trouble free gardens for us. We can have decking, patios, water features and gravel areas to cut down the amount of watering we do. Every town has a garden centre where we head on Sundays to congregate with our fellow garden worshippers and commune with the great God Mother Nature. Gardening books compete with cookbooks for the leisure reading of the middle classes. It was never like this because the garden always used to be a place where families grew their food.

My Mother had an Uncle Will who lived in the Somerset Town of Street. He was her Father's brother. Will, and his wife Lil, didn't have what we would recognise as a garden, they had a yard. In the yard was a sty for the pigs, a chicken house, and large areas of ground for vegetables. Uncle Will was very proud of the fact that he had never in his life eaten anything frozen or from a tin. I can't imagine many could say that today. Around the yard were a series of sheds with lasts. A last was the foot shaped piece of metal used to make shoes. Street was the home of Clarke's Shoes and the entire Town was involved in the manufacture of shoes. They were often made by outworkers, who worked in sheds behind their houses. Around the yard were various fruit trees including a cherry plumb, which was unique to Somerset. Backing onto the yard was the house and garden of their daughter and son in law, Peg and Percy and their son and daughter in law Terry and Wendy. All their names were abbreviated giving Will and Lil, Peg and Perc, Tare and Wen. And they were all self sufficient in fruit vegetables and eggs and self-sufficient in family support and counselling. If Tare and Wen's children needed to see their grandparents or their great grandparents they just wandered across the yard. It was the Last of the Summer Wine; it was the last of true family life as it was in the centuries before depression was invented to keep us all entertained.

The garden I grew up in was a generation on from Uncle Will's pre-war garden but it was still a place where the principal function was growing food for the family. We had an orchard with apples to cook and eat cherries, pears and plumbs. We grew soft fruit by the ton. Strawberries, raspberries, gooseberries, blackcurrants, the list was endless and there was always something ripening ready to eat. You don't need me to tell you how different supermarket food is. Everyone seems to accept this and we know that nothing will change. There was no processed food, no food in film covered containers, no preservatives, colourings, added salt, nothing was sugar free, there were no E numbers. How we poison ourselves now and what a terrible effect it has. We also didn't need gymnasiums to keep fit. A spell digging in the garden was enough!

My Mother rarely strayed into the garden, so it was the one place we could be happy. We fly to Disneyland for an escape to a children's fantasy land but in the garden we created our own. There was a sandpit for little children, trees to climb for older ones, paths to cycle round, a lawn to play clock golf and a twenty yard strip of turf to learn cricket on. The garden gate provided a goal for football in the street. A lamppost provided a rugby post for practising place kicks. A shed provided a hut for my gang to meet in, I organised puppet shows and most fulfilling of all, my friend Bill Dosser and I built and raced our soapbox carts made from pram wheels and old bits of wood. These were truly happy days and I defy anyone to argue that anyone could be happier with the plastic toys and outings to theme parks that children have today. We had a freedom that's been lost forever. We had to create our own fantasy world of cowboys and pirates. We created our own sport. There were no girls in this world. None of the boys in my road seemed to have sisters. Girls were an altogether hidden and mysterious bunch who played no part in a boys play world. There was one girl in our village who would allegedly let you go down the fields with her for exploratory activities, the idea of which filled me with equal measures of horror and curiosity. I never availed myself of this facility for fear of being sinful, so don't know how true it is!

The high spot of the year was when the combine harvester passed by the house on its way to the field at the bottom of the road. This was so exciting. The corn was harvested in such a way, that they always left a square of corn in the centre of the field. This last remaining area was filled with rabbits, hares foxes and mice. When the combine went in on its last run we formed a circle to give chase to the foxes. I remember following one, which stopped and hid behind a straw bale. I gingerly tiptoed up to the bale ready to do what, I'm not sure. When I got to the bale the fox had vanished into thin air. It was a magical disappearance that defies all understanding. Cunning creatures, foxes.

When the combine finished, all the boys in the village helped lift the straw bales onto a trailer and the hugest treat of all was being given a lift back to the farm sitting on top of the straw. Health and Safety and farm mechanisation has stopped all of this but for centuries this was how boys were introduced to the only work available, working on the land. I imagine my Granddad had the same fun working on his Uncle Jonas's farm in Devon. Not many realise that the long summer holidays, which are such a tradition, came about because children were needed to gather in the harvest. They now have organised and documented work experience in offices to fulfil the same function. But not half as much fun!

There were still horses working on the farms but mainly pulling carts and trailers. I always longed to be able to ride a horse, inspired as I was by the TV adventures of the Lone Ranger and Tonto, ('yes Kemosabe,' said Tonto with suitably subservient monotony). At the field at the bottom of our garden was a retired Hunter (a horse used for hunting). I one day went up to it to stroke it. It moved and stood on my foot and nothing I could do would shift it! It was very painful and I wasn't so enthusiastic after that!

When darkness began to fall we made our weary way back home to our mothers. The final meal of the day was always tea. This consisted of sliced bread, with home-made jam, lemon curd or sandwich spread. The only cooked meal we had was lunch. We usually had our tea on folding card tables in the sitting room so we could watch the telly! And yes, in many ways they were happy days. What a shame I should grow up feeling so badly about myself. How sad that I never remember the garden. The pain of the kitchen and the loneliness of the bedroom far outweigh anything else.

The boy who chased the fox I now recognise as little dick. He got lost. He gave up chasing foxes but never gave up wishing he could. Writing this has helped me remember that it wasn't all bad. Life isn't like that. It's just that the bad bits obscure the good bits and part of being healed is valuing and recognising the good bits, bringing them out into the light of day. Leaving the sadness of life indoors and finding your child in the garden and letting it play. Chasing foxes. The old house may be wrecked but there's always the garden.

CHAPTER 3 GROWING UP

There laid in a grave, a person I had killed and it was a terrible thing to have done what I had done. I couldn't believe that one-day someone wouldn't notice him gone and wonder what had happened. They would question me and what would I say? Should I own up? Was it an accident, or worse, was it deliberate? It was such a long time ago.

Victims of childhood abuse have many similarities. They grow up feeling worthless. They blame themselves for what they see as their failures. When the parent is the abuser they try harder and harder to win the love that's denied them. They do all they can to please the abusing parent, to win the love and affection that's denied to them. Nothing they do ever comes near replacing the love they should have had. I was 33 years old before anybody told me that I was a success. It was the person shortly afterwards was to become my ex-wife, who told me that I wasn't the abysmal failure I had felt all my life. I was stunned by the news. Like someone telling you that you had two heads and you'd never before noticed.

As a middle-aged man I learned that Mrs. Palmer, my Primary School teacher had told my Mother when I was little, that I was bright enough to go to Oxbridge. Nobody ever mentioned it to me, so I settled into a childhood of what appeared to me to be, staggering mediocrity. Yet I had learned to read and write before I was 4 and had started school at about the same time whilst others my age were playing in their sandpits. I had a beautiful soprano voice and was angelic enough to appear as a full front page in the Leicester Mercury in my surplice surrounded by holly and Ivy. The Christmas Edition. So angelic that readers asked for more pictures, which were published the following week. But nobody mentioned it. Of course, I forgot. My brother might have been upset.

It seems unbelievable now, but as a small boy I was dressed in the National costume of Austria and Bavaria, 'lederhosen,' which were short trousers made of leather. This was the 1950's when all things German were hated and despised. You rarely saw a VW beetle on the roads but if you did it was a strange sight, this car which symbolized the Nazi party. So, here was I, from the age of about 4, till about 11, whatever the season, whatever the weather wearing leather trousers. I have to say that I didn't mind at all. I didn't realize how strange I would have looked, and how contemptible. I may as well have worn a brown shirt and a swastika armband! It was the Broughton family against the world. Leather trousers were highly practical for a boy given to climbing trees and making dens down the fields. They could never be dirty, never needed washing, and never needed mending. As I grew each year a new pair was purchased on our annual holiday in Austria.

The family holiday was a great adventure, which we all enjoyed. Even my Mother. It was usually a mood free time when she was happy and relaxed.
Going to Austria wasn't that easy in those days. There were no airplanes to speak of and no motorways except a few in Germany. The journey

took three days there and three days back, all meticulously planned by my Father. He didn't drive so my Mother drove whilst he navigated. I usually sat between them on the front seat on my Mother's hand luggage. Seat belts were unheard of, as were disc brakes. It was amazing that I never plummeted through the car windscreen! I remember one time trying to persuade my Mother to try our new Ford Zephyr's maximum speed. With 4 passengers and luggage for 2 weeks holiday we managed 100 mph, but not for long.

My brother had an encyclopedic knowledge of cars and could keep us all informed about the foreign cars which we never saw in England. My Father had a driving licence but only drove on one occasion when Mother was feeling ill. It was on an Autobahn in Germany and in those days they had huge potholes. He thought it was best to steer round the potholes thereby making the journey smoother. It made us all feel so sick my Mother decided she was well enough to drive after all and we all felt a lot better after that. Europe was filled with the military, mainly American. I remember that one day we stopped in a lay by for a cup of tea, which we made on a camping stove, we carried everywhere. A US Army jeep drew up and parked next to us. The soldier opened up the bonnet and took out from the engine a tin of beans, which he was heating up there.

Our journey often took us through Germany where we visited people my Father knew before the War. In those days there was hardly a building that didn't bear the scars of wartime bullets. They still had rationing on the continent and we would smuggle tea under the car seats. I was strictly forbidden to mention this when the border guards checked us out. Little did they know. I remember once visiting my 'Aunt' Gisella in Holtzminden. Her garage housed the chickens, which had a subterranean run, from the garage under the back garden to a small enclosure at the end of the garden. It was very impressive. Chickens aren't as stupid as you think!

We once stopped in the village of Dachau and looked through the wire at where the Concentration Camp had been. It was so quiet. There were no birds singing. Nothing. Just silence. Chilling.

The holidays were spent walking in the mountains or with me fishing in the lakes or swimming when I wasn't fishing. Talking to Austrian boys while I fished I picked up enough German to be fairly fluent, particularly about fishing!

I'm not sure how we crossed the Channel in the early days. I have a vivid memory of our car being driven onto a net, and winched up by a crane then lowered into the Hold of a great ship. Later we drove to Southend where there were wartime Dakota transport planes that flew cars and their passengers across to the Continent. The Airline was called 'Silver Wings,' and on one occasion my Brother and I were invited into the cockpit with the pilot. We climbed down into the Hold with the cars and then up a ladder. It was very exciting! I remember there was water sloshing about where the cars were stored which was a little worrying! I shall never forget seeing a man on a bicycle in a Southend suburb through the window as we climbed into the air. The man became smaller and smaller and I thought about how his world was so small and the real world so big. Many years later a Medium told me that that is how spirits see the world. They can see what's round the corner but they can never be sure what's going to happen. They see the bigger picture, which we can't see.

I also remember stopping on the journey back from Southend in Cambridge. Seeing the great edifice of Kings College never dreaming that one-day I would make it there.

I started at a small village school. I was allowed to visit before I was old enough but only unofficially. I couldn't be put on the register. I walked there and back with my brother. As far as I can remember there were no school dinners or packed lunches. You walked home for 'dinner' and back again in the afternoon. It was about a mile which meant hat from the age of four I walked at least four miles a day. What a contrast with the lives of children today.

There were no indoor toilets. Just a wall, open to the elements, and a gutter, with two cubicles for the girls who had to scurry past the boys, busy at their 'wall.' A visit to the toilet in winter was a challenge particularly for the girls who had to disrobe more than the boys!

There were two classrooms. One for the infants and one for the juniors. The rooms were arranged in rows leading back from the front, one for each age group. If you were say, 8 years old, you had a blackboard in front of your row with your work on it. When you'd finished you could do the work on the next blackboard for the 9 year olds whilst the 7 year olds were on your left able to ask you to help with the work on their black board. It was a wonderful system, which allowed each person to find their level and find help from older children if they needed it.

There were cloakrooms with pegs for your coat and PE bag. For PE you had to walk in a crocodile to the top of the village to the Village Hall. The 2 strongest boys would be charged with carrying a large wooden box carrying the 'apparatus,' which included bean bags which we used to throw at each other. I think we were supposed to. I was enormously proud of the fact that the handles on the box came from my Dad's shop.

Here is a picture of the wonderful Mrs. Palmer. Rosie Roberts is second along from her on the back row. David Brooks, who bullied me, but just the once is between Rosie and Mrs. Palmer. I am at the end of that row looking rather tubby! Russell Washington Collins is there with his distinctive bow tie just below me. Next to him is my greatest ever friend 'Doss.' I still have the scar on the bridge of my nose where apparently he had thrown something at me. Funny how I don't remember that. Little Phillip Bentley who died shortly after this picture was taken is the small boy in the front row. Bear in mind that this wasn't the picture of one class, it was the entire Infants department!

The juniors were taught by Mrs. York. When I was little I had a lisp. People were for many years amused by the story of how I was sent by Mrs. Palmer to see Mrs. York for some more chalk for the black board. I was supposed to have said, 'thick thicks of white chalk pleath Mith York,' and caused considerable amusement but I have no recollection of it!

In the juniors we went to the local park for 'sport'. With just one teacher for the 30 or so juniors and a female at that, Mrs. York organized rounders for the girls whilst the boys were supposed to organize football, or cricket in the summer. The major part of football in the winter came with erecting the goalposts. This was a major undertaking and when we had done it we spent the remainder of the time, 'resting.' One boy was the lookout. When Miss York was seen coming over the horizon we quickly started a game, invented a score and she never guessed that we had done nothing apart from 'rest!' Our soccer skills remained largely undeveloped!

There was a boy called David Brooks who once pinned me up against the wall and frightened me but apart from that it was a blissfully happy and fulfilling life. I was quite lucky that 'Broughton' is one of those few names that doesn't rhyme with anything otherwise I would have been called names. I was in love with a girl called Rosemary Roberts. We were such good friends. I always preferred the company of girls and never really understood what boys were all about. I'm the same to this day. Maybe it was having a distant Father I despised and longing for a female closeness which had been denied to me. More probably it's because girls are so much more grown up. Boys seem only interested in sport, cars and work which sadly don't inspire me much.

Tragedy struck the life of young Rosemary as first her Mother died from cancer and shortly afterwards her Father died too. She and her brother Tim had to live with their Grandparents. It was very sad.

When I was ten a sort of tragedy struck my young life when it was announced that the village school was to close, being 100 years old, and the pupils transferred to a modern school not far away. It was a particular tragedy because we were learning our multiplication tables at the time. Each pupil was given a hurdling athlete made of card, which symbolized where you had reached in the race to get to 10. I had reached midway between 5 and 6. The school closed before I'd done 6 so I taught myself my six times table. I never did 7, 8 or 9 so to this day I can only tell you what 7 times 8 is by doing 6 times 8 and adding 8. We hadn't done joined up writing either and I never did manage it!

At about this time Miss York told me a very shocking thing, she said, 'you don't want to believe everything you read in books you know.' I was appalled at this. It must be true because Mrs. York was always right. But I felt as if there was nothing you could rely on, nothing at all you could trust. I was also totally shocked when she would have it that a tool I knew to be a chisel was in fact a screwdriver. I couldn't even trust Miss York! The world was becoming a totally unreliable and unpredictable place.

Now in those days the 11 plus exam ruled supreme sorting the small amount of wheat destined for the Grammar Schools from the vast amount of chaff destined for the secondary moderns and a life in trade and industry. My Mother decided that the local school was not good enough and I'd have no chance with the 11 plus if I went there. So I was sent to a school three miles away in Leicester. John the Baptist Junior School. I was never consulted about this decision.

I was desperately unhappy there having been uprooted from small village life and all the familiar people and places I knew.

It was at St John's, my new school, that I created my protective shell. My own little world where I was safe. Where no one could hurt me. I suppose we all have one, more or less. You couldn't trust books, parents, the Education Authority who close your school. Trust no one.

The school was streamed into two classes. Those who had a chance of passing the 11 plus, and those who didn't. As there was only one spare place in the school and that was in the lower class that was where I was placed and that was where I was bored stiff and friendless.

Here is a picture of me, sitting just in front of the two girls at the back in my first year at St John's.

Notice the wooden desks on a cast iron frame. They were very uncomfortable!

My Mother was told that, contrary to her expectations I had no chance in the 11 plus. She complained and had me moved into the upper class for my second and last year there. There was no spare place, so I had to move around the class sitting where someone was away until eventually someone left and I was given my own desk.

I hated playtime and usually stayed in the classroom. There I made friends with some of the girls who seemed to like me including Audrey Wood who I rediscovered many years later through Friends Reunited. I fell in love with Vivienne. She had the desk behind mine. She was dark-haired, dark eyed and just the most beautiful ten year old you ever saw.

I remember so clearly taking the dreaded 11 plus. My Mother told me 'you can only do your best' which was an enormous comfort to me. As if 'my best' would be permissible then it didn't matter if I failed. My best had never before been good enough and was never good enough ever again. I remember the exam itself as if it was yesterday. There was a math's paper one-day and English the next. The math's paper started with a simple multiplication. I couldn't do it and got very flustered so I remember thinking I would start with the difficult questions at the end of the paper first and work backwards through the paper finishing with the easy ones. This must have been an unwitting masterstroke, as most people never reached the difficult questions at the end of paper getting bogged down with the easy ones.

The English paper consisted of an essay. They gave you the first sentence, about a boy running away from his home on a cliff top by the sea, and then the last sentence about the boy returning home at night during a storm. Everyone did a story about the boy running away to sea. My story was about the boy wanting to go to University to Oxford, being given a lift by a Gentleman in a horse drawn carriage. The gentleman told the boy that the only way of getting to Oxford was to work hard at school and pass his exams so he returned home one stormy night! What a creep but it obviously impressed the examiners!

I don't know what proportion went to Grammar Schools but it was quite small and there were only 3 Grammar schools in Leicester any way. Of those passing, the elite went to a school called Wyggeston boys. It was a very successful school in many ways sending more boys to Oxbridge than almost any other school in the country. Apart from, that is, Manchester Grammar. In other ways it was very poor. The non-Oxbridge people were just ignored and left to fester. Bearing in mind that none of my family including my Father my brother and my cousins had ever passed the 11 plus not only did I do well to pass, I did even better to be chosen to go to Wyggeston. So why did I feel it was all a terrible mistake and they had only let me in because my Father had gone there (as a paying pupil)? Why did no one say 'well done'?

Others I knew who had passed were given big presents, like new bikes. I was rewarded with a visit to see South Pacific at the cinema. With my brother. And we were going anyway. I was pretty hurt but didn't say anything. But then I never did.

But I did feel that I didn't fit in. I felt I didn't belong and yet again I felt very lonely cut off from the friends I had made. Worse than that. For the next 10 years I would be cut of from all feminine contact. Many years later I would write the poem, 'Girl on the 31 bus' which showed my longing for some female contact.

When I was young, I fell in love,
With the girl on the 31 bus.
Her hair was long, her face was sad,
Just the slightest trace of a bust developing.
But there she was, and there was I,
In love with the girl on the bus.

We never talked, we never spoke,
How I ached for the chance of romance developing.
What do you say, how do you talk,
To a girl you have seen on the bus?
Had she noticed me? What did she think?
Would she be interested in a boy with acne developing?

I never knew, never found out,
What life would be like with the girl on the bus.
Never found the words. Never was that brave.
What chance I missed, never to be kissed,
By the girl on the 31 bus.

I wonder where she is today,
The girl on the 31 bus.

She's 54, and looks it too, a sagging waist,
and crows feet developing.

Children of her own, grandchildren too.
Perhaps she takes them for a ride to town,
Together on the 31 bus. And remembers the time,
When she was young, ignoring the boys on the
bus.

Wyggeston School was on a site which came into
existence during the First War as a camp where
shell shocked soldiers home from the War were
sent. The Army had built rows of temporary huts,
which later became our class rooms. Underneath
the paint on the doors you could see 'Ward'
followed by a number. My Father remembers being
taken there when he was little to stare through the
railings at 'the poorly soldiers.' Hope they put up a
good performance for him. All the schools I went to
had air raid shelters. They became useful storage
rooms for sports equipment and places for boys to
go for a secret cigarette. The handles on the doors
turned anti-clockwise to open which was the
opposite way to normal. It was said that they were
designed like that because the mentally ill couldn't
work out how to open them so were effectively
locked in. We all believed this, which shows the
level of ignorance, which the world needed to grow
out of in the ensuing fifty years or so.

I was desperately unhappy in my first year at
Wyggeston. I couldn't do most of the work
particularly the Latin. Our Latin Master was the
appropriately named, 'Tombstone' Greaves. The

History Teacher was similarly named 'Snotty' Hailwood!

If you lived 3 miles or more away from the school you could have a bus pass. We lived 100 yard short of the 3 miles so at first I had to cycle. I never questioned why I couldn't be given the few shillings it would have cost to go on the bus.

I was never picked for the football teams that played in the playground at break time. I felt like telling them I'd been the First Team Captain at St Johns, but I never could find the words. Perhaps they somehow knew that the St John's team I captained had played an entire season without winning or even drawing a single match. I did score one goal that season but I have to confess that it went over the bar and the ref missed it. When I think back, I had never even seen a football match played by anyone apart from my school friends. There was no football on TV and I never went to see 'the City' (Leicester City Football Club) because of my brother's passion for Rugby and the Leicester Tigers (Rugby Team).

I hit on a plan of telling the other boys that I was really a Red Indian descended from the Apaches. Fortunately I never carried through with this plan. I just wanted someone to be interested in me. I did however eventually make the School Rugby team which put you amongst the elite of the elite. I had been dragged by my brother every Saturday from about the age of seven to see the Leicester Tigers so I had a good grounding in how to play. Our very Welsh Rugby Master was very impressed with my fearless tackling! One of our teachers was Mike Harrison. I had no idea he was, at the time an England International and captain of the Tigers. You can't imagine Will Carling or Johnny Wilkinson being a full time teacher and the pupils not knowing how famous they were. How times have changed.

After the first year we were 'streamed' into 5 classes of 30 in each. I avoided being put in the bottom one, which would have been quite a disgrace. But not for me the high fliers who were destined for Oxbridge who were fast tracked into a class called 'the remove'. How grateful I was as they were all fearfully bright!

I was encouraged in my belief that I had hidden powers when I was caught on camera by the local paper with a Goldcrest. They spookily refer to me as Richard Broughton.

The aptly named Mr. Otter referred to in the article worked on the Ironmongery counter at Broughton and Jones and was also my Father's like long snooker partner. They played at 'Osman's' a disreputable snooker hall behind my Father's shop used by rogues vagabonds criminals and footballers if those classes are mutually exclusive which they are probably not!

So school life passed quite happily and I was successful at Rugby and nothing else. I performed moderately at O'Level and entered the Sixth Form.
I was down to do RE or 'Divinity' as it was called. Geography, which I loved, and Economics. Somebody miscalculated and there weren't enough desks in the Economics room so a volunteer was needed to do something else. I volunteered, as I had no interest in Economics. On the spur of the moment I decided to do English. Probably the best decision I ever made as the English Teachers were

inspiring and taught us to think and form our own opinions. I loved English.

During my first year in the sixth form I devoted my entire energy into my band We were called 'Smokestack', and our advertising pronounced that we were 'Exponents of Rhythm and Blues.'

Here is a picture of me on the left looking uncannily like Marc Bolan before even Marc Bolan was Marc Bolan. History doesn't record how successful were Marie and Eunice Drew but I we must have done better than them as we won the contest and went on to tour with the legendary 'Christian St Peters' he of 'Pied Piper' fame!

THE TALENT SPOTTERS

Marie and Eunice Drew, of Rosamund Avenue, Leicester, a close harmony duo at the audition.

One Leicester group featured at the audition was the Smoke Stack. Left to right in the picture on the right are Steve Broughton, Dave Harris, Bryan Atkins, Jim Coley and Terry Abbs.

awards

I had more fun with 'Smokestack' than anything before or since. The Beatles had transformed the world and we could have been next in line. We could have been except I did very badly in my end of year exams and decided to give up playing in the band to concentrate on becoming a Theologian. Bizarre I know. At the same time I had an encounter with a hairdresser who persuaded me to have a proper haircut. Underneath the shaggy mop was a rather smart looking young man as you will see from the next photograph taken about a year later.

The band member standing next to me was our lead vocalist and harmonica player Dave Harries. He eventually went to Hornsea College of Art and devoted his life to drinking and living off benefits. That is real rock and roll.
He became very deaf and lived in Scotland restoring antique furniture. Don't breathe a word to the DHSS! Sadly he missed the one and only band reunion by inconveniently dying the week before it was due to take place. The only other traceable band member failed to turn up as he had to take his wife to work on the night shift at Asda!

I really wanted to read Theology at University and applied for various Bible Colleges not realising that they were training people/men for the Ministry. I never applied for University and to this day I don't know why. I believe it was because no-one at school thought I would get in. So, after the A' level results came out and I'd done rather well there seemed to be nothing left to do but go back to school for a third year in the sixth form. This was for those retaking failed papers and those applying for Oxbridge. As I hadn't failed anything there was nothing to do but apply for Oxbridge. I was not expected to succeed especially as the minimum entry requirement included having an o-level in a classical language, Latin or Greek which I hadn't got.

I was very lucky to have an inspiring teacher we called 'Holy Joe' Mr. Arthur Ireson. Unknown to me, my Mother had taught his children, twins, and he seemed to think he owed her a favour. He decided I would go to his old College St Catharine's, Cambridge, to read Theology despite my protestations that I couldn't do Latin let alone Greek. In those days the minimum entry qualification included a classical language. He hit on the idea that I could learn Hebrew as Hebrew was inescapably a classical language. I had just 3 months to achieve this. On my own with no one to help. He got me a book and I started off. I learned the alphabet and I worked out that if I earned about 5 words per day I might just know enough to get by. Luckily Hebrew has no grammar to speak of. No gender and even the letters double up as numbers and even words! For example the letter 'B' or Beth as its know is the number 2 and it also means 'house' as in 'Bethlehem' or house of bread. Easy peasy!

There was another small obstacle. You had to take an entrance exam. Unfortunately the Theology entrance exam required a knowledge of both Latin and Greek so that was out! I set about to study for the Geography paper. I was offered an interview and off I went. Feeling a total fraud and impostor but with a 'nothing to lose' approach, off I went. You had to spend the night there, in the College, which was difficult as I couldn't fine the toilets and was too afraid to ask!

I was interviewed by a Cambridge and St Catherine's legend Dick Gooderson.
We agreed that there was no point me taking the Geography exam and had a very pleasant chat about the Master of the College's sick goldfish. I was something of an authority on goldfish at the time. He seemed suitably impressed.

A few weeks later a letter came from Cambridge. We had moved to a chalet bungalow, which had belonged to my Grandparents. My Bedroom was upstairs and my Father came up the stairs with the letter. He turned and was going back down the stairs when I told him what the letter said. They were offering me a place to read Theology on condition I passed O-level Hebrew. His only words to me were, 'well that's that then' and he continued down the stairs. His son had been offered a place at Cambridge and that's all he could say. I was never going to pass O-level Hebrew so 'that's that then'. End of story. It was as bad at school. Mr Ireson was beside himself with joy and I was summoned to the Headmaster. His name was Larkin but known by the boys as Druel! His listened to what I had to say in total disbelief. 'Bring the letter in and I will read it, he said, or words to that effect. The next day I took the letter in for him to read. It was only about three lines long and after an age he uttered the unforgettable words, 'well, that's what it seems to say.'

At Wyggeston, getting into Oxbridge was the big thing. As places exhibitions and scholarships were offered announcements were made in assembly. The Head Boy then stood up and shouted, 'School' will you stand please. Three cheers for our latest award winner, Hip Hip etc etc etc.' My place was never announced and I never had the three cheers.

Next January I sat alone in a room at school sitting O-level Hebrew. Mr Ireson was the invigilator. After about an hour he announced that he was 'just popping out'. Having 'popped out' he returned carrying a tray of biscuits and fizzy drinks. It was an amazing act of kindness by a truly great man who changed the course of my life and inspired me to achievements unheard of in my family.

Later that year I learned that I had passed O-level Hebrew with flying colours although by then Cambridge had dropped the entry requirement and I could have been admitted without it. I never lost the feeling that I somehow got in by the back door ahead of others far brighter than me to do a subject that nobody else wanted to do. And most painful of all I never escaped the feeling that for some reason my Headmaster and even my Father felt that some great injustice had been done. As if people like me shouldn't get ideas above our station.

When you get a place at Cambridge the world changes very dramatically. I entered a world where I felt I didn't belong. The same as I felt at St John's.

The same as I felt at Wyggeston. Along a road leading where I didn't want to go with people very different to me. From homes very different to mine. But I never wanted to go back to the world I had known. What drove me forward was simply a desperate need to escape. So escape I did.

CHAPTER 4 CAMBRIDGE

It was said at the time that Cambridge was one of the first areas to have its' gas supply converted to Natural Gas because of the high suicide rate amongst Undergraduates. People would literally put their heads in gas ovens and die. It was thought that it was because of the high expectations of families putting pressure on young men (mostly at that time) who had probably reached the limit of their potential. And maybe it was arriving at Cambridge, having been at the top at school and finding that you were only average. For me it was simply the isolation and loneliness coupled with an amazing amount of work, all to be done to tight deadlines. For the first time I started wishing I was dead. A feeling that has never left me.

I was put into digs about three miles from the College. The geographical limit of what was thought acceptable. The house was beyond the bridge along Mill Road and backed onto railway sidings. Not many people know how much shunting of engines and rolling stock goes on through the night. I did! Night after night. The house was a tiny terrace. The room I was given was so small the bed folded up against the wall. When the bed was down the room was filled. To get to the toilet you had to go down the stairs through the living room and through the kitchen of the old couple who lived there. The lady was totally deaf. I would sit in my room all evening desperate for the toilet but not able to face the ordeal of the journey through the private lives of these total strangers. I did though have the trusty transistor radio and the pirate radio stations so that was some comfort. I also had my Dansette portable record player and my assortment of 45 records.

Life in College was no better. I was the only Undergraduate reading Theology so I not only knew nobody but it was hard to get to know anyone. The evening meal was a formal 'hall' with waiter service, but that was out for me, as I had no one to go with or to sit with. Lunch was self-service cafeteria style so if I arrived early I could sit by myself and not feel so lonely. Not feeling as if everyone was staring at me wondering who I was. I couldn't afford breakfast. So in my first term I rarely managed to eat, lost weight and my hair fell out in chunks. It also seemed to rain and rain and rain without ceasing. Cycling three miles there and three miles back in the rain was not great.

After a while I made the discovery that I could by a loaf of bread and some butter and live on that. It was like a King's banquet! I had no access to a fridge so the butter was difficult to keep!

I had my first slipped disc at the age of 11 but I'd developed a severe slipped disk problem in the 6th form, so playing Rugby was out. I would like to have learned rowing but that was out too, though I doubt I would have liked it. Not a place for the Grammar School boys with chips on their shoulders about Public School boys! So I took up sailing. I hated it with a passion but it got me out of Cambridge for a few hours on a Saturday, which was good. I knew nothing about dinghies and dinghy racing was quite beyond understanding for someone brought up as far away from the sea as you can get in England. A race was just a period of time when I was shouted at and froze so much my body was racked with the pain of chilblains. Wet suits were out of the question. The person driving the thing would shout, 'leeow,' or something similar and I was never quite quick enough.

Eventually my body packed up and I was found in the College library rigid with pain from a slipped disc unable to stand up, or walk, let alone cycle.

The College found me a room in the college. I couldn't have a bed in the sick bay as there was someone with an infectious disease there. I was given pain killing injections which made me very ill and then morphine injections which made me very…….floaty! I was also given a board for my bed, which was a great help. I kept that board for many years and in time it served as a kitchen work surface!

At this point in my University career things started to look up!

It's funny how I have to be at rock bottom before anything changes. As if my fairy godmother only steps in when she knows I can't take any more.

The room I had was part of what was called a 'set'. Two rooms, with a shared kitchen and bath. I was to share with a guy called Trevor Fishlock. Trevor saved my life. He was a scholarship boy from Southampton Grammar. Possibly the most gifted Physicist at Cambridge at the time. Or possibly not, but he was my hero! He had a broad Hampshire accent and the most wonderful friends from Southampton. When I was fit enough I now had someone to go to meals with. They were mostly engineers. Not particularly intellectual, not at all scary!

My room was over the kitchen at the junction of Queens College, Kings College and my college, St Catharine's. One day as I lay half-paralyzed in my bed, I noticed a sign in the room in Queens that overlooked mine. It read, 'Get well soon!' It was very kind and very moving. I was beginning to feel less isolated and alone.

One 'floaty' Saturday afternoon as I was enjoying the effect of the morphine there was a knock at my door. I was too floaty to answer but the door opened and in walked the person who was to share the next 13 years of my life and with whom I was to have my most precious daughter Harriet.

She was a fellow Theologian and had come to borrow something. Her name was Vanda and she came from Colchester. She knelt by my bed very tenderly and we were to become the very best of friends. Real soul mates. She was friends with Priscilla Chadwick, the most famous female of the time at Cambridge the 'Rag Queen' and the two of them would help me hobble down to the river where they would take me for rides in a punt.

I had suddenly arrived!

Here's a picture of us at St John's College May Ball 1998. Quite the suave and elegant couple! Vanda made the dress herself. She ended up with a First and is a lecturer in Librarianship at UCL.!

At the time there were only three colleges for girls who were accordingly in short supply. In the Theology faculty there were just two girls and they were now both close friends of mine. Before we 'met' Priscilla and Vanda had thought me aloof and 'above' them. Nothing further could there be from the truth. At the end of lectures and supervisions I had always sped off without chatting to people. It was because I was desperate to get to lunch as soon as it opened. I didn't think anyone was interested in me. They thought I was a high flyer with no time for them!

As my mobility improved I spent more and more time with Vanda and we became an item. More of that later.

I began to enjoy life at Uni as they now call it and to enjoy Theology. I must mention the legendary 'Mrs. N,' or Mrs. Northfield to give her a full title! She was a 'bedder,' a lady employed by your College, who made your bed and sorted you out. She was extremely kind and cheerful and made my life much happier than it would otherwise have been. Having a female in your room after 10 p.m. was an offence the College could sack you for, and it was usually the bedders who gave the game away. Mrs. N. was the soul of discretion and would even leave two cups of tea outside the bedroom door in the morning. Bit of a giveaway that I suppose but very kind for all that!

One of the luckiest things ever to happen to me in my early life was meeting the Reverend John Sturdy, the Dean of Caius College. A truly wonderful man he was actually interested in what I had to say. This was the first time in my life anyone listened to me. I suppose some people go a whole lifetime without anyone caring enough to listen. For me it was a great boost to my rather precarious self-esteem.

He was a brilliant Old Testament Scholar. He decided to learn Danish as there were some un-translated books by a Danish Scholar about the Old Testament he wanted to read. Publishers paid him to produce English versions being the only English/Danish bi-lingual Theologian. I proofread some of his translations but the work was meticulous and faultless.

John and I continued our friendship long after I left Cambridge. He invited me to College dinners and always made me feel that I was an interesting person. He once came to London and we had lunch at Law Society Hall in Chancery Lane. I was deeply embarrassed that he expected me to pay for both of us and despite digging deep and using every available luncheon voucher I had to ask him to contribute the shortfall. This was pre-credit cards. I remember him asking me if the firm I worked for had a room where the staff could have their tea. In all my working life I have never heard of such a place! He must have thought that offices were a bit like Colleges. Little did he know.

I must have been quite good at Theology as I earned a 2.1 in my first year and the same again in my second year, narrowly missing a first. For a boy from Leicester who struggled to pass O-level this was a monumental achievement. Vanda was a typical Girton girl. Intellectually in a different league from the rest of the world, let alone Cambridge. Look her up on the Internet at what she has achieved if you don't believe me. When I told my Mother our second year results all she said was, 'you didn't let her beat you did you?' as if it was an egg and spoon race. This was so cripplingly painful when I was desperate for some word of encouragement. In one crushing phrase she destroyed the feeling of achievement and self worth I was entitled to and it took a lifetime to rebuild the damage she had done. Maybe others wouldn't have taken any notice, but for me it was a terrible thing to hear your Mother say. How are you to take your place in the world and embark on adult relationships when you feel such a failure? In a very real way my Mother stopped me growing up. Maybe that was what she wanted. To keep the parent child relationship, because she couldn't imagine any other.

I think it was then that I finally cut off all emotional ties with my parents. Never again would I be their son. I was sick of being used as something to brag about with their friends and family, 'Steve's at Cambridge' swank swank, and all the time they could never say to me 'well done.' It would have cost them nothing. I know that many young people suffer far greater abuse at the hands or mouths of their parents and that comparatively speaking I have nothing to complain of. I didn't come from a broken home, I wasn't physically abused and I was fed and clothed. There were many happy times and in many ways my Mother was very supportive. She helped me with my Band, she watched me play football and rugby whenever she could and I know she would be shocked to know what I was experiencing. But that's the point. She didn't for a moment think about what her children needed. How they felt. She was aware of my brother's anger and would often ask me why I thought he was the way he was, I didn't know then but I do now. She never seemed to be aware of my withdrawal from her and the world in general. She was obsessed with her own needs and her own unhappiness. It may be that her unhappiness was a symptom of the world not feeding back to her, the affection she needed. You need to love and to be loved in return. A narcissistic world is ultimately an unhappy one because if you can't be loving to others, they can't be loving or giving to you. Perhaps there are many like her, perhaps many children are affected in this way. But if you are, it doesn't occur to you that your sadness isn't normal. It isn't your fault. You are a victim. You were being damaged and you had no way of knowing it. It's a curious feature of abusive relationships that the abuser isn't always aware of the damage being caused and the abused person thinks it's their fault! I could imagine the majority of abusers being narcissists but then I find it hard to imagine people being innately evil, as no doubt some people are.

My Mother lived in a world with her at the center. The world only existed in so far as it affected her. She was totally incapable of seeing anything from anyone else's point of view. Incapable of imagining how anyone else felt. Incapable of seeing how she affected others. She was never wrong. She even knew what you were going to say before you said it. She had the infuriating habit of finishing your sentences for you. She once said that the theory of evolution was nonsense. 'If humans were descended from apes then there would be apes turning human all the time.' It sounds stupid and on one level it is, but she wasn't stupid, she just believed she was better than Darwin! She once went to South Africa at a time when apartheid was at its' most severe. She thought it was a great idea, 'you see, the blacks smell terribly, you wouldn't want to sit near them, so we don't sit on their seats and they don't sit on our seats. If there aren't any white seats we don't sit on theirs.' Again, she had no way of imagining what it would be like to be black or coloured in a racist regime. She did think it was bad when the South Africans didn't allow Basil D'Olivera to play in the England Test team but even then, she couldn't condemn apartheid!

My Mother went to Church every Sunday at 8 am. She never missed. On the way back she always called at the same shop which was run by an Indian gentleman. She always spoke about him with great affection. Our birthday cards always came from his shop, not particularly tasteful. I mention this because I don't think she was racist in the normally accepted meaning of the word. In the last few years of her life she was cared for by a Sikh lady who got her up, washed her down and made her breakfast for her. Mother was very fond of her. But, as I said before, she could never imagine what prejudice and problems the immigrant community might have had. What it was like to be an immigrant. What it was like to be her son, her husband, her friend.

So, at the end of my second year at Cambridge, I started to think about how I would make a life for myself. I couldn't see me becoming a Vicar or earning a living from Theology, so I thought I'd have a go at Law. I discovered that if I did one year of law, then six months at the College of Law, I would then have all the exams I needed to be a lawyer. If I failed then I hadn't wasted much time.

So, without telling the now hated parents, I quit Theology and took up Law. It was a doddle. So easy compared to what I'd been used to. I had no great aptitude for it and no real interest in the subject. I scraped by doing the minimum.

Doing a different subject brought me in touch with a whole new circle of friends. I really liked Bob Winstanley. A long haired, bearded undergraduate at my College who had converted from doing History. He was altogether brighter than I was and after a successful career with his own legal practice in Islington he became a Judge. His wife Jo became a good friend too. I was now half of a couple, friendly with other couples. I was best man at their wedding and very proud of that. Bob was friendly with Edwin Shirley whose Father owned a lorry. He would lend his Father's lorry to Bands or 'Groups' as they were called in those days. The lorry expanded into several lorries and became the Edwin Shirley Trucking Co. Their lorries driven by 'hippie' drivers took the Rolling Stones and all the big name bands around the World. When BBC arrived in Suffolk with a Radio 1 outside broadcast it was Edwin Shirley who provided the transport. Makes you feel particularly unsuccessful when people you know are that famous and famous for doing what they love.

There were several boys from my school who went to Cambridge at the same time. I was closest to

Peter Honour who read English at Queen's. He had been awarded an Exhibition and had a brilliant mind. He, like many others couldn't cope and had a breakdown.

As you will see from this article he and I, with his friend Richard Coleman filled in the time between School and University by going on a bit of an expedition. More of a holiday really. We did coincide with an earthquake in Turkey although we were asleep at the time. There was also the Seven Day War between Israel and everyone else in the region. The illness referred to was Richard being overcome by heat stroke. The dignitary handing over the award was later to reappear in my life in a small but significant way!

THURSDAY, SEPTEMBER 28, 19

PUFFIN AWARD COMMEMORATES A BRAVE MAN

PARENTS of Old Wyggestonian John Hoare, who died last year while trying to row the Atlantic in the boat Puffin, were at the school speech day yesterday to see an endeavour award commemorating the vessel's name given away.

Mr. and Mrs. J. R. Hoare saw the award presented to two sixth-formers for an expedition by van this summer to the Holy Land.

The boys, F. S. Broughton and P. J. Honour, received the award from the Lord Mayor of Leicester, Alderman Sir Mark Henig.

The headmaster, Mr. J. C. Larkin, in presenting his annual report, said: "This must be a day of mixed feelings for the parents of John Hoare, but I hope they will gain some consolation by the knowledge that his endeavour is commemorated in our prize list.

"I am sure that they will be pleased to know that we had nine worthwhile entries," he said.

In their expedition to the Holy Land, the winners were to some extent hampered by the Middle East War, the Turkish earthquake, and illness.

P. J. Honour (left), and R. F. S. Broughton — the winners of the John Hoare endeavour award at the Wyggeston Boys' School prize distribution.

I remember visiting Peter in Fulbourn psychiatric hospital. He was on Valium and Librium. This was my first experience of mental illness and the start of a lifelong involvement with the mentally ill.

My friend Stephen was at my College about 10 years later and he too ended up in Fulbourne. He was part of that elite among Cambridge Undergraduates who was destined to receive a 'First,' a First Class degree. Only a few in each subject were ever awarded each year so you were the best of the best. Three weeks before his final exams he suffered his first uncontrolled bi-polar episode. He locked himself in his room and wrecked everything that was in it. Everything. Tiny pieces. He was eventually persuaded to open the door to be met by two Doctors who dispatched him to Fulbourne, where they signed the papers to have him, 'sectioned,' He was allowed to sit his finals whilst under heavy sedation and still under a section. Twelve months later he was to sit his final Law Society exams to become a Solicitor when he lost it again in Guilford High Street and was taken by the Police to the local Hospital to be sectioned again. Another life ruined by pressure and perceived parental expectation. Like most parents they adored their son and simply wanted the best for him. Like many parents they had no idea what was best for their son and no way of finding out. You love your parents. You want what they want and try your hardest not to let them down. And you let them down retreating into mental illness where you hope people will feel sorry for you and take care of you, a damaged child. But what do they do? They can't accept or understand the illness and encourage you back onto the road well travelled that's supposed to lead to success and happiness. It doesn't. It's the road, the journey, that makes you ill. Stop the World; you really need to get off. Leave the planet. Stephen didn't want to leave the planet. He created a 'box' in which to live and felt safe there. Dying would mean leaving the box and that was very frightening. Better to trust the box you know than the box you don't know.

One of Peter's friends from school was John Coral. He'd been School Captain at Wyggeston and was at Christ's. He decided that being at Cambridge was a wonderful opportunity to become educated and he decided he didn't have enough time to waste it being with us. He was probably right and I am sure it stood him in good stead for later in life. Most people will tell you though that you learn more at University from the people you meet, than from the text books you read! It was about this time that I decided that I too was fairly uneducated. I thought I should read some books for the first time in my life. In my younger days I had raided my Father's store of paperbacks and read several 'War' books, mainly novels about the exploits of prisoners of war. I took myself to a bookshop and found the Penguin Classic series. I thought it would be logical to start at the beginning with Jane Austin and work my way through the alphabet. As I didn't fancy Jane Austin, I then thought I would start at the other end and work my way backwards. I read the entire works of Emile Zola and a few by Israel Zangwill and then gave up! That was the extent of my literary education whilst at University but if the author has a name beginning with the letter 'Z' then I'm an authority.

John Taylor was another school friend and he was at St John's. His dad was a tallyman, if I remember correctly. In the days when there was no credit, the tallyman would buy things for people, using his own money and then collect the money for the goods on a weekly basis making a living from the interest earned. He could buy things at a discount from most shops. The tallyman was put out of business by the mail order catalogue, which operated in the same way.

John graduated and went to work in a bookshop and as far as I know, spent his whole life there. Nothing wrong with that. I wonder if he got as far as Emile Zola. Probably not!

When it came to leaving University I knew I couldn't go back to Leicester but didn't know how I could find the money to live for six months whilst at the College of Law. Vanda decided to become a Chartered Accountant. Their training was different and she would be earning from the start. We decided that she would support me for six months until I could earn. I wanted to stay in Cambridge but Solicitors outside London didn't pay their trainees so you were expected to support yourself. It was a profession for the sons of rich men. Mainly for the sons of solicitors.

Undergraduates didn't work to support themselves as they often do now. You had a grant. This was means tested and because my Dad's income was above a certain level I didn't receive a full grant. The parents were supposed to make up the difference. Mine didn't and that was very hurtful. They found the money to buy things for my brother but there was never any money for me. My Mother was in the habit of bringing food parcels, which I deeply resented. She had not only given me nothing, not even a word of praise, she had taken from me my achievements and made them her own. She had taken what little status I had and made it her own. When she tried to put her arm round me it was for her benefit not mine. She was always robbing me, stealing from me and there was little I could do to stop her. She would try to kiss me and I really hated it. It was like being raped. I was in a very real sense systematically abused. Not physical abuse but psychological and emotional abuse. Stripping all my self-respect, all my self-confidence and all my feelings of self worth. 'You didn't let her beat you did her' turned a huge success into a failure. That sense of total failure stayed with me all my life. And worse than that, it drove me on to work harder and harder so there was no fulfillment only more urgent need for achievement. I ran a marathon and felt a failure so I ran nine marathons in all and always felt I'd failed. Years and years pounding the streets in the cold and dark. Runners always talk of that wonderful feeling crossing the finish line. I never once experienced that.

On graduation day you had to invite your parents. We stood outside the Senate house in Cambridge where the ceremony takes place. It's also the place where the exam results are posted. My Dad was reading all the results. Looking for someone famous. Instead he found my name. 'Says here, you took Law'. 'Yes I did, I changed last year.' My mother replied without a moment's hesitation, 'I thought you would'. She could never imagine there was anything she didn't know about so that was it. Of course she had known.

So my idea became her idea. My decision became the fulfillment of her prediction. My life became her life. The theft of my own life was total. It belonged not to me but to her. I had no thought, no free will, no feeling. I was a non-person. I may as well have been dead. Dig the hole, put him in, throw away the spade. Goodbye Dick, hello Steve.

And my Dad? Well he was a person who wanted to go home as soon as he'd arrived. And how bad did that make you feel?

CHAPTER 5 LOVE AND MARRIAGE

The man in the white coat had taken my dog away and she never came back. Why didn't anybody tell me what had happened? Why did nobody care what I felt? Why couldn't we have another dog? Why was the pain at that loss unnoticed? You learn that nobody cares so although you have feelings you daren't express them, there's no point. They transform into feelings of being defeated. You look to your Mother to see how it should be, to be a guide, a friend. I didn't have that. To tell you that you're OK. It's OK to have feelings and to express those feelings.

If you grow up feeling unloved you grow up feeling unlovable. You can only believe that there's something wrong with you. If anyone wants to offer love and affection to you, even a simple hug, you feel they are trying to take something from you that you don't want to lose. So the prospects of having a fulfilling relationship are remote. You cringe and draw away at every hug, every peck on the cheek, even a handshake is something to avoid. You avoid contact even with your own children. You never have affairs even though you might like to. You never pat a passing bottom. Most important of all you never complain.

I often think about Rosemary Roberts, the first person I felt something for. I was about 5 years old. When her parents died she became a sad thing. Many years later I was working in a filling station and she came in with Mrs. Bradley, the owner of the local Riding School, a very butch sort of person.

They were in a Morris Minor pick up which had no oil in it's engine. Mrs. Bradley wondered if this had anything to do with the green light! Rosemary didn't recognize me and I didn't speak to her. She still looked very sad. I couldn't tell her what I would have liked to have told her. That she had meant the world to me and being separated from her had made me feel very lonely.

The first girl I ever went out with was the strangely named Jennifer Bumford. We held hands but never kissed. We went to dancing classes together. I learned the traditional ballroom dances, the Gay Gordons, the Valetta, the Waltz and also some modern ones, the Twist, and the Locomotion. We shared moments on the dance floor, like overhearing a girl say to her partner, 'now this is my right foot and this is my left foot.' Some times we would go to the cinema taking the last bus home. I loved the walk from her house to mine, about a mile, and I often used to run it. The cool night air made running so easy. I enjoyed being a 'gentleman.' My Mother had taught me to open doors, to walk on the outside of the pavement, to offer my seat on a crowded bus, always to carry the shopping. Jennifer probably thought I was mad! Even now I like to treat a woman like a lady and feel uncomfortable if I don't.

She eventually wrote to me one day, telling me the family had acquired a beagle puppy and she didn't think she would have time to 'go out' any more. Jilted for a dog.

My next romantic adventure was with Elaine Dennis. She taught me how to snog which we did regularly on her doorstep, until she wrote to tell me that her boy friend, who was in the Army, was coming home on leave and she couldn't see me anymore. Jilted again. His name was Steve too. This was not doing me any favours. I did though, thoroughly enjoy the snogging and will always be grateful for that.

Next came Dorothy. I was 19 and she was just perfection. She had the most beautiful Auburn hair, and a beautiful figure. She gave me the greatest of gifts, a love of classical music. On second thoughts, and being brutally honest about this, the greatest of gifts was being allowed to grope her young body and her ample bosom! A love of classical music was a poor second!

We sat together listening to Romeo and Juliet, just loving it. But her greatest love was Sibelius. We spent hours lying together enjoying the music. Having learned Tchaikovsky and Sibelius I discovered Bach and Bruckner and a lifetime's pleasure opened up before me. I owe it all to Dorothy. We were 'in love' or as close to it as you can get at 19 but we met just before I went to Cambridge and having then met Vanda I decided that there was no future in a relationship when she was going to University in Sheffield. There were no mobile phones, no text messages, no transport apart from that provided by parents. So I broke it off with heavy heart as although Vanda had become a good friend I still felt I was in love with Dorothy. Many years later after years of searching, I found her on the Internet because I wanted to say sorry. She didn't respond and I felt very sad about that. She's married with two children and teaches at a school in North London.

I had no idea whether I was good looking or not and never felt worthy of anyone's affection. I was a committed and devoted suitor but never ever felt loved.

I had no sex education at all. I remember at the age of 10 wondering how babies got into the world. My Mother told me that when there was a Mother and a Father and when they were both very happy they knelt down and prayed to Jesus who gave them a baby. Some boy at school told me that babies came out of a woman's bottom but I found that difficult to believe. I eventually found a diagram in a Tampax box in the toilet and it all became a little clearer! At school Holy Joe Ireson was in charge of sex education. He had in interesting idea that homosexuals could be divided between 'verts' and 'perverts.' Verts were those who were born with their wires crossed, i.e. it wasn't their fault. Perverts were those who were perfectly 'normal' but took it up as some sort of twisted hobby. I think that many people share this twisted sort of logic! There was a Catholic boy in my class who asked Holy Joe if you catch a venereal disease from your wife. He seemed to think that it should be medically impossible, because of the sanctity of marriage. The boy was Jim Gannon and years later I saw him on 'Top of the Pops' playing guitar with a Band called 'Fox.' They had a hit with a song called 'Sssingle Bed.' Jim went on to have a career in pop music and now lives in Australia having played with some very famous bands in his time. I often wondered if that could have been me, or Dick. Probably not!

One of the teachers at school told us that sex was very good indeed which whetted our appetite. Being at a boys only school and then at an all male college my sexual encounters were strictly limited. Dorothy let me feel her body which was extremely pleasurable and I eventually had sex with Vanda when I was about 20 but never managed to make her at all fulfilled or satisfied which led me to believe that I was pretty rubbish at it. No one will ever believe that we had a marriage lasting 12 years with no 'physical' side as it is euphemistically called, but it was true. And we never talked about it either. Here I was with intense feelings of unhappiness totally unable to talk about them and not knowing why nothing 'worked'. But if you never show your feelings you can't begin to have a relationship and you get angry that she can't guess what the problem is which to you is bloody obvious. And all you can do is to try harder and harder to be a kind caring husband. And nothing works. We created a paradise together, a moated Suffolk farmhouse set in three acres, horses, dogs, chickens, ducks and a beautiful daughter. It was to become Paradise Lost and broke my heart in the process.

Our family Doctor when I was young was Jewish. Dr. Korn. He and Mrs. Korn also a Doctor had escaped from Germany before the War. My parents were in awe of him. He had delivered me and saved my life in doing so having the cord around my neck. For reasons that were never clear I'd been circumcised as a baby. I blamed Dr Korn! As a result I was always embarrassed at my 'condition.' I avoided being seen naked at all costs. When other boys happily had showers after Rugby, I quickly dressed and disappeared. Not only my name was taken away from me, something others had was taken too and just added to my misery.

How can a person who is dead become a good husband? The person that killed him can try as hard as he likes but it's all pretend, it's all a sham. Try mending a roof with just your bare hands. You need something to work with.

Vanda and I had our honeymoon in Norfolk. We visited a number of churches rubbing brasses which was our hobby at the time. Motoring down a country lane I recognized a car coming the other way. It was my Mother. Hundreds of miles away from Leicester, she just 'happened' to be in the area. She managed to take my honeymoon away from me.

About 10 years later our daughter Harriet was born. I have heard people talk about the birth of their first child being the greatest of all life's experiences. If it is then again those feelings were drowned in a sea of sadness. She was born by cesarean section. Fathers weren't allowed in the Operating Theatre in those days. You were told to keep away from the Hospital until after the operation was finished. I remember being shown into the room where she'd been placed after the op. She looked so perfect, so peaceful, so still. The nurse asked me if I'd like to pick her up! I was horrified, why should I want to pick her up? Feelings that were very confused. What a rotten person. I have always found it difficult to express the feelings that I know I have. The feelings that everyone else has but which others seem able to rejoice in. Your first child. A daughter, and yet, you feel confused. The feelings you have are drowned in the misery of being trapped in a relationship that wouldn't work, that couldn't work. A relationship that was bound to end in tears.

At the christening Harriet started to grizzle and my Mother grabbed her and whisked her away to the back of the church. She couldn't let anyone else be the center of attention. She wanted to be the star of the show. Poor Harriet even missed her own christening. At our house afterwards we were having the traditional christening tea when my Mother decided she would 'clear away'. This was before some of the guests had arrived. She had ruined the christening and the party afterwards by her own jealous selfish behaviour.

Vanda and I decided to have nothing to do with her ever again. So for nearly two years I was rid of her. One day in the middle of all this she decided to descend on Vanda when she knew I was at work. She wasn't going to be separated from her Grandchild and rather than try to mend fences she was going to take the barricades by storm. To her credit, Vanda gave her a very impressive talking to about how appalling her behaviour had been but she just couldn't believe that it wasn't just Vanda who was upset but me as well. She went home but never said 'sorry.' That would have been impossible and she was prepared to lose contact with her son and granddaughter rather than admit she was wrong.

After leaving Vanda I re-established contact but I wasn't brave enough to mention what had happened and she therefore won another victory, I suffered yet another crushing defeat.

My closest friend as I was growing up was a boy I called 'Doss'. William or 'Bill' Dosser was his real name although the boys at school often called him 'waterworks' because he cried so often. We went everywhere together. Often spending all day 'down the fields' making dens, pretending to be Robin Hood. Well I was Robin Hood, Doss was a merry man!

With the 11 plus came the parting of the ways. He went to Secondary Modern I went to the Grammar School 3 miles away. Leicester is a big City. Wyggeston took young boys from a huge area. There were no Wyggy boys of my age from my village so it was all very isolating.

I can honestly say I never had another friend after the age of 11. I could only relate to girls. Boys were a mystery to me and still are. I know a lot of girls who say they prefer male company but never have I heard a man say he prefers the company of women. I do, and probably always will. As a married man it's almost impossible to have female friends.

Going to University meant I lost contact with Doss who became my brother's friend. I was pretty sad about that. After our Father died my brother gave Doss Dad's snooker cue which I had really wanted. All I had of his was his electric razor. Mother had no use for it. I threw it away as I had one but kept the electric flex, which was better than mine. All I inherited from him was a piece of electric wire. That, and a total inability to stand up for myself and be myself.

After my marriage to Vanda came to an end I became incredibly lonely. I had had no contact with my parents for about 2 years. I wrote to my Mother to tell her and she told me that before she had received the letter she had felt as if a great weight had been lifted from her. Another way of saying she knew in advance what I was going to do. I was not allowed to make any decision of my own.

I suppose this Chapter is a bit thin. No sex, no love and no marriage. But then that was the story of the first 30 years.

I did eventually find all three, which was how I began to rebuild the house and bring back to life the person I had killed. But at the point in 1983 when my world collapsed for the first time that was how it was.

I must give credit to a Scottish Lady called Margaret Blakey. I met her at that time and she managed to extract from me through gritted teeth how unhappy I was. She made me realize that I just couldn't carry on. She told me that I had to learn to enjoy being by myself before I could start enjoying being with someone again. I never managed that although it was good advice. I thought she and I could build a life together but it wasn't to be. She had Kevin unbeknown to me and that was the end of that. Everybody, including Vanda though I wanted a divorce because I was having an affair with a girl at work. Nothing could be further from the truth. When you feel as badly about yourself as I did there's no way you have the self-confidence to have an affair. You just wish you were dead.

I was separated from little Harriet who was two years old. It was her second birthday that persuaded me that I couldn't carry on. Vanda opened a card in which a friend had written, 'I bet you'll be having a lovely time with a party, jelly and ice cream.' We weren't. It was a miserable day and I thought to myself that I couldn't bear to bring up a child in an unhappy home like mine had been so the only thing I could do was to leave. I thought so badly about myself that I thought I would do them both a favour by getting away. I know now how terribly wrong that was.

People who commit suicide often believe that the world will be a happier place without them. They say so in the notes they leave behind. I felt the same. Looking back I know that's just the product of a distorted self-image. Children want both their parents to be there even though they might hate each other. I remember on her third birthday, she wanted us both to take her to the seaside. We did but it was very miserable. Miserable for us. Not sure it wasn't miserable for her too. I shall never forget standing there on the shingle beach staring at the cold North Sea wondering why it had all gone so horribly wrong.

And the wind blew through the holes in the walls and the rain came through the roof and a lonely shallow grave lay unattended, hidden, secret, ashamed.

CHAPTER 6 THE SPIRIT WORLD

Once when I was a teenager, I was lying in my bed, and I found myself 'flying' round the room. It was a wonderful sensation. I couldn't go very fast but I could maneuver round corners well enough without bumping into the walls.

I often tried to repeat the experience but only managed it on one or two other occasions. I doubt that you'll believe me. There's no earthly reason why you should and there are probably other explanations for what was going on.

But to this day, I am certain in my own mind that although my body remained in my bed, some part of me, possibly my 'spirit' became detached and could float free. Sounds cranky I know.

Since about the age of 11 I've suffered from a bad back, or slipped disc, whatever you prefer to call it. I occasionally went to a 'quack' physiotherapist, Mr. Westwood who manipulated my spine and tried to bring some relief. One day I went there, I was about 18 and in the 6th form and when I got back to School I began to feel faint and eventually passed out. An ambulance was called and I dimly remember being loaded into it, people talking about me having stopped breathing. My parents were called and they rushed to the Hospital. The journey from school to ambulance wasn't very long but along the way I suddenly found myself floating about, near the ambulance roof looking down at my body. Holy Joe was by my side and seemed to be saying prayers.

As I floated about it all began to go misty and swirly and I remember thinking, 'someone will be coming for me'.

No one did, and I woke up in Casualty with this nurse asking me 'did he walk on your back?' I assured her that he hadn't. I sat up and made my way out only to meet my anxious parents who had now made it to the Hospital. From that moment on, I knew that not only would a part of me, and a fully conscious part as well, survive bodily death and decay but that it would be a wholly pleasurable experience. Wishing I was dead, became a real alternative to be looked forward to. I also knew that I wasn't going to be allowed time off for good behaviour. I was here to stay and there was no escape. They would come for m when they were ready and there was nothing I could do about it.

Apart from the bad back, the other strange feature of my physiology has been my susceptibility to fainting. I faint on a fairly regular basis, usually without any particular reason. I hit my thumb with a hammer. I fainted. I saw an eye operation on a TV in a Chinese restaurant, 'your life in their hands.' I fainted. I went to the Doctors to have a BCG test inspected. I fainted. I was in Church one day and singing a hymn, I fainted. The list is pretty endless. I know I'm going, I can be sitting down, standing up, having a meal, watching TV. I just faint and it takes forever for me to come round. I usually know I've fainted and have some awareness that I'm out of it, but there's nothing I can do about it. It's like someone upstairs decides to bring me in and my body is left helpless whilst my consciousness is whisked off somewhere for some unknown reason.

The most spectacular incident came whilst I was lying in bed one night. Fainting is quite different to sleeping and I knew I was fainting. An ambulance was called and it was thought I'd had a heart attack. I was admitted to hospital and put on a monitor. Very strange that, seeing your life reduced to a trace on a screen. Comparing your trace to others on the Ward. If it stops you know your time is up!

Once they get you in a hospital it's hard to get out. Unless, that is, you can persuade them you're mentally ill! They told me it takes three days of tests to tell if you've had a heart attack or not. I'd had enough of being in hospital, so persuaded them to let me out after the three days which they did on condition I had a treadmill test, to test my heart during exercise. I was in full marathon training at the time and fancied giving it everything on the treadmill. Wrong decision. I'd finished the test and they were taking off the electrodes when what happened? I fainted! So I was readmitted back to the Ward I'd just escaped from.

Eventually a big wig Consultant from Papworth told them I was 'vaso-vegal.' It had a name, my condition. Translated into English, 'vaso-vegal' means you faint a lot! Brilliant!

Being in hospital taught me a lot. I slept with three grandmothers in one night, which must be some form of record!

It also taught me that wearing hospital pyjamas destroys your morale and will to live. With shorts and tee shirt you might just survive the system. More to the point, you can make yourself feel better if you concentrate on helping people worse off than you. There are plenty of those. There was one lady on the Ward who wanted a cup of tea, which she could only sip through a straw. The only problem was that she wasn't well enough to hold the cup properly so she just lay there, not complaining while the tea got cold, just because no one had the time to hold it for her. So I did. That made me feel so much better, just doing that.

After a week in Hospital I was let out and thought I'd go for a run. I took about 20 steps and had to give up. Hospital destroys your fitness. If you're not fit when you go in it would seriously damage you!

My Mother had 'healing hands.' She had an Aunt who was a village healer in Somerset when she was young and the Aunt told her that she would inherit the gift when she died. She felt that healing was somehow against the teaching of the Church so she rarely practiced it. There was therefore no challenge to her basic theory about herself. Like saying you could run 100 meters in less than 10 seconds but you don't want to.

It goes without saying that I never let her put her 'healing hands' on me. In fact the only healing she did was on poor Uncle Arthur in Kettering who had a steel plate in his head. As I mentioned he ended up killing himself in the boating lake in Wickstead

Park. Now when I say, 'never' this was true until a few years before she died. It was Christmas and my 'slipped disc' was agony. I could hardly move and I knew she would offer to give me a 'rub'. I thought that if I let her it would in some way break the barrier that existed between us so I let her. Much against my better judgment. The result was unfortunately astonishing. A great heat came from her hands, which became redder and redder. She eventually had to stop as her hands were hurting so much. My back pain disappeared and never came back to that part of my spine. I had to admit that cranky though it sounded, she had a very powerful gift of healing. She said that when she died she thought the gift would pass to one of my children. One of my daughters is training to be a Doctor but being totally scientific in outlook I doubt she would ever have any truck with healing hands.

The dearest friend I ever had was a man called Hugh Stibbe. It was a brief friendship really. We worked in the same firm for about 4 months and kept in touch on the phone occasionally meeting from time to time. He had a brilliant mind. An Oxford graduate he qualified as a Doctor and then gave it all up to become a Solicitor. He had been a very wealthy man with a family engineering business. His brother lost all the family money with bad investment decisions leaving Hugh virtually penniless for the first time in his life.

He was responsible for one of the funniest things that happened to me. We were walking on a beach and our respective wives were walking some way ahead. There was a man with a metal detector on the beach. Hugh called out to his wife, 'Christine, do be careful. There are mines on the beach and this kind gentleman is looking for them!' It was one of those, 'you had to be there to understand how funny it was,' moments. The poor man with the metal detector was blissfully unaware of it all which made it that much funnier!

Hugh was however, an alcoholic.

One day, visiting his home on his birthday, he announced that he was going off to buy a Chinese takeaway. Off he went and returned about 30 minutes later. He must have bought a bottle of something potent while he was out because he came back roaring drunk. He was very loud at first then he became incoherent. After incoherence came tiredness and then he fell asleep. That was his usual pattern. It was like watching an actor on the stage. But for Christine it was an ongoing nightmare.

There is one rule about Alcoholics, which also holds good for other conditions. Alcoholics can only start to recover when you stop helping them. If they wake up soaked in their own vomit they might just wake up in other ways. While you help them, you postpone the dawning of the day when they realize how ill they are.

Hugh was fascinated by Buddhist teaching and read widely on the subject. Towards the end of his life he rather went 'off the rails' by taking money from his clients in a vain attempt to 'save' a prostitute he met in Soho. She was a heroin addict and took more money from him than he had. He bought her a house in South London and a car even though she didn't drive. Before he was found out he had a heart attack and died. As he lay dying, his wife Christine comforted him with the news that an ambulance was on its way. 'You're not taking me to any fucking hospital', he said, whereupon he died. I think they are the most wonderful 'last words' anyone could possibly utter.

Christine asked me if I would go to a psychic medium to see if we could 'make contact' with him. He believed totally that there was indeed a life after death so if any one would 'make contact it was him. He once told me that he thought that eternity had to be spent reliving all the experiences we had when we were alive. We'd no body to have any new experiences with so that was the only option. It followed from this that we had to cram in as many experiences as we could whilst we were still alive so as to make eternity less boring. It seems to me that this is a very sensible policy even if it wasn't ultimately found to be true! As a direct result of this policy I decided to go to New York to run the New York Marathon. When you think about it, life doesn't have many memorable experiences and sadly, it's the bad ones that are usually the most memorable.

Because Christine had asked me to, I went to the most famous psychic medium in the area. She lived in a weird little ramshackled house with a weird husband in a poor part of town. She sat me down and I offered her a lock of Hugh's hair, which Christine had given me.

I was ready for some generalized, non-specific 'message' but totally unexpected for what was about to happen. Her first words were,' there's a word which means something to you which means nothing to anyone else'. She paused as if she was listening to someone telling her. 'That word is…'semper.' Now that word won't mean anything to you as she predicted but it meant so much to me. 'Semper' is Latin for 'always' and is part of the motto of Leicester City, 'Semper Eadem,' always the same. It's on every bus, every dustcart, every Council lorry and it always made me smile to myself, 'what a crummy motto, always the same, never getting any better.'

And when I came to Ipswich, my walk to work took me past Ipswich School which has a large heraldic crest on a side wall. Underneath the crest are the words 'semper eadem' and every day I used to say to myself, 'just like Leicester, always the same never getting any better.' But how could she have known that? Nothing had been further from my mind at the time and I'd certainly never spoken about it to anyone. Spooky or what?!

It was telling me that this was for real. Not a freak show, a trick, a gypsy fortune teller at the fair. There was something very remarkable going on which couldn't be explained away.

She then told me that there was someone there who 'had been poisoned in his body and poisoned in the air.' How disappointing after a great start. Hugh had a heart attack. She was quite insistent. 'There's some money missing, you're helping his wife and trying to find the money. This was truly astonishing. It wasn't Hugh it was a client called Steve Byam who had committed suicide having stolen money from his employers the Ipswich Port Authority. He had taken a paracetemol overdose and put a hosepipe to his car exhaust. Poisoned in his body and poisoned in the air.

She told me he was in an agitated state and didn't trust women. I asked if he could say where the money had gone and the message came back that his friend Pete had it.

Several weeks later I met his wife in the street, and asked her if he had a friend called Peter and she told me he had and who he was. They had been in business together in a Tool Hire company. I couldn't mention the encounter I'd had with the medium. Further time passed and I was asked to attend a Creditors meeting of a Tool Hire company at the offices of Grant Thornton the Accountants in Ipswich on behalf of one of the creditors. I went and it became clear that Steve Byam had supported his friend and their company with stolen money, which was now irretrievable.

Back to the séance! Having received the messages from Steve, she found Hugh. The way she worked was to have a cassette running to record all the messages. I gave the tape to his wife Christine and she was totally astonished at what was said. It didn't mean much to me but it all made sense to her. His message to me was to tell me that our third eye covered up during our life in the material world is uncovered in the spirit world so we see things with greater understanding. I hadn't known much about this third eye but Hugh being an authority on Buddhism would have been fascinated by it.

She then told me that there was a young girl with a message. She had been in an accident with her sister when she died but her sister had survived and she wanted to tell her Mother that she was OK. She knew I hadn't known her but said that my firm was connected with the family. This meant nothing at all
To me but I later discovered that it was a daughter of the famous Ipswich Croyden family. They'd had a large Jewelry business in The Town Centre for many years and Mrs. Croyden owned a small shop, which I used to visit most days.

I never did have the courage to go to her a total stranger and tell her I had a message from her daughter but many years later I did learn from a close friend of hers that she had been visiting mediums. I never found out if he had passed on the message.

When I think about this experience, which I have done a lot as you can imagine, I know with a profound certainty that the world of Spirit is very active in our lives. That death is not an end but a beginning. And there is nothing to be afraid of. It was the same with my near death experience in the ambulance and my floating round my bedroom. If I do anything with this book I hope it will persuade a few people not to be afraid.

When you open up yourself to talk about things like this it is truly amazing how many people will share similar experiences. So much so that I now believe the world of spirit moves me towards certain people and certain people towards me. So much so that I will never refuse help to anyone. I never refuse to speak to any one on the phone. I always make myself available to anyone who wants me to help them and I always accept invitations to go places and do things that normally I wouldn't dream of doing. There is always a reason behind it and always some good to be done. Take my meeting with the publisher of this book. I am a Trustee of a local charity and have been for many years. They always have a speaker at their AGM. I went along when it would have been so much easier to say I was too busy which I was. Speaking at the meeting was a representative of this publishing company. Some inner calling made me go up to him after the meeting had ended. He gave me his e-mail address and the result is what you now have in front of you. I don't have to write a book but feel that someone 'out there' wants me too,

For many years I've presented the 'Morning Thought' on BBC Radio Suffolk. More of that later but just to say the same thing applies. Being Radio you never know who, if any one, is listening, and you wonder if you can think of something interesting, entertaining and thought provoking. I used to thing that someone 'out there' used me as a channel and I was happy to oblige. They were good because the BBC keeps asking me back. It seemed unfair to take the credit for it when my input seemed so negligible but in this skeptical world that's how it has to be. I'm not sure that I believe that any more. It may be because I have such a poor self image that I couldn't believe I could do anything good without a lot of help.

A listener once wrote in asking if she could have a copy of my reading of the poem Dover Beach which I had set to music for my Sunday Morning spot 'words and music'. She had recently lost her husband. That morning she was in the kitchen and she heard his voice telling her to turn on the radio. She did and at that moment I was reading that poem. She wrote that she and her husband had done their 'courting' on the beach at Dover and my reading of the poem had brought back many memories.

The most moving and perhaps the most convincing experience of the world of spirit was told to me by a wonderful Glaswegian lady called Sylvia Shahat. She was married at the time to an Egyptian. He was Shahat Shahat but I digress! She had been working as a nurse in Glasgow and caring for an elderly gentleman whose dying wish was that he should be buried in full highland dress. She was happy to oblige when the time came. She had finished the job when she noticed that there was no kilt pin. She couldn't find one anywhere so she went and bought one, fixing it to the kilt just before the coffin lid was closed for the last time. Many years later at a spiritualist church in Ipswich the medium said that she had a message from a Scottish gentleman. The message was simple,' thank you for the pin'. It meant nothing to the people in the church that evening but Sylvia knew exactly what it meant.

My first dog after Lightie the corgi, was an English Setter we called Sophie. Sophie was a lovely dog and I mated her to the Crufts Supreme Champion of the time, a fantastic dog called Bournehouse Dancing Master. She had a litter of 12 surviving puppies but had no maternal feelings. You had to keep an eye on her as she would often slope off and escape from feeding duties. 'Feed your puppies Sophie' I would command and she would give me one of those 'looks' to say 'OK if I must.'

She was eventually killed by a lorry outside the house but could be seen running across the lawn for some time afterwards. A few years later I went to the same kennels that Sophie had come from to buy another puppy, this time a Cocker Spaniel. The litter pressed to the front when we came to them all except one which stayed away at the back. I knew it was either Sophie or a puppy quite like her. Spaniel puppies are closely related to Setters and have the same colouring which only appears as the puppies grow older. The spaniel puppy had the same colouring as Sophie and the same grumpy personality. It was a boy we called Sydney. If Sophie had come back I know she wouldn't have wanted to be female again!

I now have a Lhasa Apso dog we call Cosmo. He too is very grumpy. Maybe grumpy people have grumpy dogs! Tradition has it that they are reincarnations of Tibetan monks although I have to say knowing Cosmo as I do this seems unlikely!

I remember a remarkable day, which was so extraordinary that it must show something significant, but I haven't yet decided what. Any suggestions will be gratefully received. In two separate incidents I saved the life on an elderly gentleman and a young toddler.

I was woken by shouts of 'fire' from my Mother in law who was staying with us. I got up and could see the house directly opposite well alight. An old gentleman lived there. I went outside to see what I could do and saw him standing in his front doorway calling for help. I went to him and carried him out of the house and away, staying with him until an ambulance arrived.

That day I was due to visit Priscilla, my friend from the Theology Faculty in Cambridge. She was now the Head Teacher of a comprehensive school in London. She'd been married to an opera singer for about a year but had never remarried or had children. I drove down to London, found where she lived and parked the car. I got out, locked the door, and there standing in the middle road was a little girl no more than two years old. I scooped her up out of the way of oncoming traffic and took her to the pavement. My immediate thought was that someone would think I'd abducted her. But where would I take her? I decided to stay where I was until someone appeared. No one appeared! I saw that the house I was outside had an open garden gate so I took her in my arms and went into the garden. There she was greeted by what must have been her Father, the one who had doubtless left the gate open, who took her from me. I'd saved his daughters life but received not a word of thanks. Just another job for........Super Solicitor!

Priscilla wasn't at all pleased to see me so apart from a bit of life saving the journey was wasted.

My Mother firmly believed that when she died she would see the children she had had but who had been either miscarried or stillborn. The strange thing was she made me promise not to tell my Father she had told me about the miscarriages and the still birth. She seemed to have been ashamed but then again she may have made it all up just to gain attention. I shall never know.

My Mother had for many years a cleaning lady called Mrs. Anderson. She believed that her spirit left her body when she was asleep and went around the world doing good things. To me, that falls in the category of 'crank' belief. But she also told me that every night when she was little her grandmother kissed her good night before she went to bed. One night no granny, so she asked her Mother what had happened. Her Mother told her that her grandmother had died before she was born. Could that have been true or just a fantasy?

But what good is it all, this talk about spirits and life after death. Do the spirits talk to you through your dreams? Do they make things 'happen'?

I was once loaned a Book called 'A Course in Miracles'. If you ever meet anyone who has read it you can be sure they are a very special person. In many ways the most valuable thing about the book is the first page which says simply words to the effect, 'miracles happen when you stop believing in coincidences'. These are the most powerful words in the Universe and I would urge you to remember them and put them into practice. As a result my life has been one long miracle. Not a day passes when I am not made aware of the force of this way of thinking. Was saving two lives in one day a coincidence, just happening to be in the right place at the right day or was it a miracle?

The existence of this book and my meeting with the publisher can only be described as a miracle, far beyond coincidence. And does it matter where the power behind these miracles comes from? I suggest not. If you prefer, think of the mind like a great computer. There is software which allows you to type a page of words but all the time running in the background is another type of software making a million decisions every minute which keeps the computer running. It's called of course Windows and is very clever indeed.

I think the mind is like that. Take a simple act like crossing the road. You look right and sometimes left and see the road clear and off you go. But while you were doing that, the mind was doing a lot of other things you weren't aware of. Calculating speed of traffic, calculating distances. Working out when it would be safe to cross. Listening for things unseen by the eyes. Activating the muscles that get you across. It's called the super conscious mind and it is far more powerful than the conscious mind. This super conscious part of the brain is what some call the soul and some call the spirit. It's that part of us we all suspect exists, but which can't be contacted by the conscious mind. I believe it can communicate with other super conscious minds and we call it telepathy or intuition. It can make accurate assessments of people on first meeting. We call it 'gut reactions'. I suspect that mediums are people who have found a way of accessing their super conscious minds giving them special powers. They visualize it as a sprit guide, often a Red Indian.

If you take away anything from this book I hope you take away the confidence to trust your intuition, to go with your gut reactions. To rely less on 'logic' and 'reason' which exist in the conscious mind and are pretty feeble. I often think that there is no point trying to make a rational decision. At any one time you only have about 50% of the relevant data so you may as well toss a coin. The greatest danger is making no decision at all. Your intuition is a product of the super conscious mind and is far more reliable.

Those dreams which disturbed me so much, were from a part of me which knew me best. Which was trying to tell me what was happening. To give me clues to a better life. The super conscious mind was erecting signs along the Motorway of life and I was ignoring them.

I am a Taurean. Read about Taureans and you'll read about me. Home loving and slow to anger. Thinking I was a Taurean type was a great mistake. The real me has yet to find out what he's like. I am slow to anger for reasons totally unconnected to Astrology, interesting though it is. There are many diversions along the road of self-discovery. Many will advise and counsel, but for me the clues were there, hidden like a sign overgrown with ivy, but they were there. Stripping away the layers of dust and debris is a monumental task. Finding Richard who sat smiling from the walls all those years, holding his duck, may be beyond me. But at least I know he isn't dead after all.

I sometimes look at my son and wonder if he is how I would have been. He does seem more real than me. Less tortured. Less damaged. I hope so anyway.

CHAPTER 7 BROUGHTON & JONES

The world of work is a godsend to people like me. You can escape from the horrors of personal life and become an actor on a stage. Playing the part. Scene after scene. Act after act. And no one knows and no one cares who you are or what you are. And no one asks.

I first entered the world of work in my Father's shop working on a Saturday and in the school holidays. It was a better University than Oxford and Cambridge put together, teaching me more about people and about myself than anything has ever done since.

My Father owned with his brother and two cousins a hardware shop in the centre of Leicester. It was called 'Broughton & Jones' and had been started by my Great Grandfather another Richard Broughton. As far I know he wasn't a 'Dick!' Big or little.

Ironmonger's shops were the same all over Europe. They even had the same smell. When I started 'in the shop' there were long mahogany counters with high bentwood chairs for ladies to sit on. The 'stock' was kept in large cabinets, so if anyone wanted say, a tea pot, you had to go to the cabinet, remove a selection and take them to the 'lady' to choose from. Having made her selection you would ask 'cash or account' and if she was, for example, a farmer's wife, it would be put in the accounts book. If not on an account you made a manual entry with a biro on a till roll and gave the lady her change. It was my Father's job to add up all the entries at the end of the day, which he did in his head, no calculators in those days, and then he counted the cash and tried to 'reckon up'. Sometimes people came in to settle their accounts, and you gave them a receipt from the receipt book. It wasn't legal unless you signed over a 2d stamp, which was brown.

My first job on my first day was to dust the stock. I remember standing on a stool to do this when a customer came up and asked me something. I had to pretend I knew what I was doing and have probably been pretending ever since. Maybe we all do.

Broughton & Jones was in the centre of Leicester. A tall, but very narrow building. My Father's department, where I worked was on the ground floor. Next along as you walked through the shop was 'the office' where my Uncle Donald worked, along a bit further was the ironmongery counter where my Uncle Bob worked later sharing it with his son Roger who still runs the business to this day. The Ironmongery department was a wonderful place. The motto of the department was 'we've got it if we can find it'. Much of the stock was kept either in the basement or on one of the upper floors. There was always a group of customers waiting to be served and no assistants serving them or at least appearing to serve them. They were usually searching for things in the basement. My brother often worked in the Ironmongery and was the victim of some friendly practical jokes, being sent down to look for 'wire netting seed,' 'striped paint' and other similar non-existent things. On one shelf was a box marked 'tenter hooks' and there really was such a hook, not that there was much call for them. The shop was in the market place in the centre of Leicester. Market traders would often come into the shop for hooks and poles, which they used to take clothes and other stock items off rails and other fixtures. I seem to remember that Gary Lineker's family were Market Traders as were Gerry Dorsey's who later became known as Englebert Humperdink! I may be wrong!

The ITV used to have a program called 'bygones', where items were presented with long since forgotten uses. Often my Father would know the use and comment that we had some in the shop. He would remember not only selling these bygone artifacts but also remember the price they used to sell at.

This was his world and had been since the age of 16. Shops were open long hours in those days and sometimes 12 hours in a day. The assistants wore brown overalls but my Father and the other Directors, his brother and two cousins wore suits as did I. As all the Directors were Broughton's he was known as Mr. Richard, his brother as Mr. Bob, his cousins being Mr. Robert and Mr. Donald. As Donald was really Robert Donald you could never say 'Bob's your Uncle' as I had three. I think that must be a record.

My Father didn't get on with the rest of the family but I'm not sure why. Robert was a very likeable person albeit rather boring and a lazy so and so, always creating new departments following his latest hobby, like the fishing department, which never sold anything justifying the time he spent in it. Donald spent much of his time 'in the office' and Bob did the travelling, to the cattle market meeting the farmers and to other customers taking orders, the job his Father had when he was younger. My Grandfather would go to three churches on Sunday and never go into any of them. To meet the farmers and take orders he would cycle to one village for 8 0'clock, see people when they went in. Then during the service, cycle to another village to meet another lot coming out. Repeating this for 12 o'clock and 6 o'clock.

So my Father perceived himself as many of us do, as the only one doing any work. He despised his brother for being a 'holier than thow' bible bashing bore although I found him to be the only cultured person in the family.

Working with my Father was Joyce Merry, an aging spinster, one of a generation who lost their potential husband in the Second World War. There was also 'Pam' who I spent a lot of time chatting to, between customers. She eventually married my cousin David who worked in the garden department in the basement. Pam was collecting for her 'bottom draw' which meant she was collecting things in advance of getting married. It's almost unheard of now as people leave home many years before marrying.

My Father was a cricket fanatic and had played First class cricket before the War. He had scored a six onto the roof of the pavilion at Lords. Even to this day an unheard of feat. He had also bowled out, first ball, the current England captain who was playing for Middlesex. This was regarded as 'bad form' as the paying public were there to see the top players perform. Bowlers were supposed to bowl an easy over to let them get their 'eye' in! This is a concept of sport, which is now totally lost.

So, being 'into' cricket he knew a lot of people in the cricketing world. I remember the Bedser twins Alec and Eric, the most famous cricketers of their era visiting the shop one day. They had a business selling or making sheds. In those days professional cricketers had to find work in the winter, so my Father would regularly employ one or two to work in the Ironmongery. I particularly remember Maurice Hallam who was a top Leicestershire batsman and occasional England player. He eventually got a job as a driving Instructor. Another was Bryan Bosher.

The garden department was run by Mr. Thornton, a man who had been a Japanese prisoner of war. He once told me that if you ever had a choice of how to die, chose starvation because you never feel hungry. You just get more and more lightheaded. I doubt that that information will ever be of any use but you never know!

This was my Father's world and he was, according to my Mother, very unhappy with it. I imagine he was, like me, an example of a passive aggressive male as he was never able to articulate his feelings about the business and his fellow Directors. His reactions were similar to mine and probably for the same reasons. Living with someone like my Mother makes you lose your self-esteem and makes you unable to express your feelings. She sucked out all the emotion from you like a vampire. She buried Big Dick and little dick!

My only memory of my Grandfather was him coming into the shop as an elderly retired man. My Dad told me he once ordered a man out of the shop, 'get out of my shop, and never come back.' I always admired him for that and wished I could do the same in my business.

From time to time a strange 'tramp' lady would visit the shop. All her belongings were kept in a large pram, which she parked outside. She would wander round saying, 'how we doin' then?' My father would follow her round making sure she didn't cause any trouble and occasionally he would wrap up a saucepan to give to her. One day she wandered into the office looking round and wandering out again. Many years after my Father died I discovered that she was a distant cousin. She was known in the County as 'Tar Oil Lil'. She made a living buying tar from gas companies, diluting it with paraffin to make a sort of creosote and people would pay her to paint their fences and farm buildings. She travelled the highways and byways with a gentleman companion living rough. A newspaper report at the time recounts how one night their shelter caught fire and they were admitted to a hospital and then an old people's home. Being unmarried they were separated so they decided they would marry so they could share a room. Very touching. Tramps were common in those days and they would journey from one workhouse to another. They were allowed to spend the night but they always had to move on never being allowed more than one night at a time. It is said that the workhouses were always placed a day's walk apart.

The Leicester workhouse was still in use as an old people's home when I was at school. It was a massive brick built building where we collected 'meals on wheels' for old people. The cooking smell in the home was as bad as the smell of the food in the containers. It was dreadful. Even in the 1960's that buildings was a really terrible, terrible, place. People today can have no idea of the appalling squalor and misery that those work house buildings must have contained. The Ipswich workhouse is still in use as a homeless families unit. That too still has an air of misery about it.

For my Saturday's work I was paid £2 which was just enough to buy a long playing record at £1. 17s and 6d in old money.

My Father and I would usually have lunch at the Chinese Restaurant behind the shop. There was a set menu costing 10s 6d or about 50p in today's money. The set menu was on a small typed menu and consisted of soup to start a main course with rice a pudding and coffee. One Saturday to my great surprise my Father summoned the waiter to explain what they had typed as the desert course. It said quite clearly, 'gooseberries.' 'What is this?' said my Father pointing at the word. 'Gooseberries,' said the waiter, in a very Chinese way. 'I don't understand, bring me some.' The waiter reappeared with a little silver bowl containing some tinned gooseberries. My Father examined them closely. 'Ah, these are Guzgogs, we say Guzgogs.' The waiter looked puzzled and handed him a pen for him to write the word down. The waiter then went round the entire restaurant altering each menu to read, 'Guzgog.' It was a side of my Father I'd never seen before or seen since. It was the Dick who had spent his youth in Hamburg playing tricks on the Professor.

A year or so later I took an exam in Spoken English, set by the Royal College of Music for some strange reason. As part of the test you had to give a talk entitled, 'At the Restaurant.' I told the Guzgog story, which caused the examiners great amusement, and I passed with a 'highly commended' Grade 1!

In the shop I learned a great deal about the general public and how diverse is the intelligence of ordinary people. That was being polite! Working in a shop you realize how stupid people can be. Another, kinder way of saying that, is how limited the intelligence of some people is. You need to know that if you're to function in a world which involves the general public.

One day a lady came in asking for, 'one of those things that go round'. I struggled to understand what on earth she might want. My Father knew instantly and asked, 'what colour?' 'White,' came the answer, and he picked up a curious little circular plastic tray called a hostess tray. You put cakes and sandwiches on it especially if you were totally lacking in taste. They were widely advertised on TV at the time. There was a choice of white or brown, but quite often people couldn't decide so you had to choose for them, depending on which colour you had the most of!

All plastic items came in a choice of three colours in those days. Red yellow or blue. Brides had to decide which of these colours they wanted for their kitchens, it was a big decision. I remember a lady coming in for a plastic bread bin. 'Red yellow or blue,' I asked. The lady thought for a while, 'lemon,' came the answer, which wasn't one of the options!

A branch of Woolworth's was nearby and people were always coming in having bought something there to buy a screw or nail to hang it on the wall. You couldn't normally buy just one nail but my Father would sell them one for the same price as a dozen, with the thought that we made more profit on the fixing than Woolworth's made selling the item itself!

I learned a lot about business and a lot about my Dad from working in the shop. I remember a traveler coming in one day trying to sell my Dad a new supply of light bulbs. 'How much do you sell your light bulbs for?' he said. 'About 3 shillings' he replied. 'Well these light bulbs you can sell for 2 shillings and 6 pence'. 'Show me some I can sell for 4 shillings and I'd be interested,' said Dad'. And how right he was.

He bought all his Christmas stock from a traveler called Mr. Duck. My Dad would go to Nottingham to sample the wares and place his order. Sometimes he and his wife would come into the shop. After many years Mr. and Mrs. Duck changed their name. They would now be Mr. and Mrs. Duke! This amused my Dad greatly.

I remember one Christmas, my Dad had bought a large number of glass ornaments which were selling for about £1. Or rather, they weren't selling. 'We'll have to do something about this, Steve.' He proceeded to change all the price labels from £1 to £5. I thought he was mad, but one by one they flew off the shelves and it was usually men that bought them. He explained that people were looking to spend about £5 on a present and anything less was a bit 'cheap'. They weren't fussy what they bought as long as it was about £5. Here was a man who knew his job backwards.

He used to delight telling people how the shop used to sell 'coffin kits'. These were sent out to farmers when someone died. The kit comprised handles, hinges a shroud and brass screws. The farmers used to make their own coffins. Men known as 'carriers' sent out the kits to the country. Each village had a carrier who would be found at a particular pub. If you had something to deliver you took it to the pub, asked for the carrier and paid him a small fee. Spending all day in a pub it's not difficult to imagine the state they were in when they got home! If they got home! If they were too drunk the horse would be able to find its way home without any prompting for the recumbent carrier.

My Father started work in the shop at 16. He would have left school at 14 but they wanted him for the school cricket team. For as long as anyone knew, it was his job to 'dress' the window. He had no great talent for this but did it anyway. It was a Wednesday afternoon and nephew Roger announced that he was going to dress the window. Dad had had enough and there and then walked out of the business that had been his life for 46 years, 6 days a week, and his only source of income. He had made his mind up. He was never going back. And he never did. At the shop it was said that he had been 'taken ill.' Others said he'd had a nervous breakdown. Whatever it was I quite admired him. To be able to get angry. To be able to value yourself enough to make a stand. All things I couldn't do.

His lifelong love of cricket set him free from a total collapse of his life. He took up cricket umpiring and never looked back. He was in great demand. Leicester has a huge immigrant population of Indians Pakistanis and Caribbean's and they were united by a love of cricket. Both my Mother and Father were latent racists. There is a large park in the centre of Leicester called the Victoria Park where a large number of games can be played at any one time. One day my Father was umpiring. He looked around and realized he was the only white man there! Not a great place to be for a person as prejudiced as he was.

The Caribbeans invited Mother and Father to their Christmas party and they thoroughly enjoyed the hospitality. My Mother enjoyed being surrounded by those tall athletic young men even though most of them were immigrants. Occasionally my Father would recognize Test cricketers playing on the park. They were usually on holiday visiting family but could never resist a game of cricket whatever the standard.

The shop was eventually sold and my Father lived on the proceeds in his retirement. My brother and I were the first generation of Broughtons since the 18th century not to have inherited a living from our Father. What we did inherit though was an inbred capacity for hard work and a love of people which is probably more valuable.

It's hard to explain what belonging to Broughton and Jones meant. My Mother believed we were almost aristocracy. Coming from a poor Kettering back street I suppose you can understand it. Status was paramount to her and she basked in the reflected glory of it all. I remember telling them of coming across another Broughton somewhere and the person said they were distantly related to the Broughton and Jones family. My Father decided that they couldn't be and my Mother replied, 'they're just cashing in on the name!' 'Cashing in,' was true fantasy stuff!

When I was at Primary School, the wooden box we carried our 'apparatus' in to the Village Hall needed some new handles. I was so proud that the new handles came from Dad's shop. At Wyggeston we did metal work and I remember making soldering irons which needed wooden handles. I was again, so proud that I could supply the class.

As a quite small boy I had to deliver parcels to people who lived nearby who had ordered things. I remember being terrified not knowing what I would have to say when they answered the door. When told, I would rehearse it over and over again making sure I got it right. It was quite good training I suppose.

This is what I remember, but what did I feel? That's harder, very hard.

I used the word 'pride' just then and that's what I felt. Pride was a forbidden thing when you went to Church, but in the context of belonging to Broughton and Jones it was permitted. My Father claimed we once had a visit from a Member of the Royal Family who parked her car chauffeured car outside but I find that hard to believe. The shop was in many ways quite famous. If you knew Leicester you knew Broughton and Jones. At some point in their life everyone had to visit it for something. There were two other Ironmongers, Pochins and Courts, (I think). Pochins was smaller and eventually disappeared. Courts were much bigger but were eventually swallowed up by a larger company leaving Broughton and Jones as the only one. Every town had its ironmongers until DIY stores took over and they were always well known. Being a Broughton gave me a sense of value and importance, which was otherwise missing. It therefore became very important to me. Sad I know, but important. I needed something to stop me feeling totally worthless. I remember talking to a girl I met at University who said that her Father had a shop in London where she worked in the holidays. 'Harrods I presume,' I said jokingly. 'No, Bourne and Hollingsworth actually,' came the reply. Broughton and Jones wasn't quite in that league!

My Brother would have joined the business either when he left school or when he qualified as a Chartered Accountant. The Uncles, Bob, Robert and Donald would never hear of it. This made Mother angry as each of the Uncles had a son in the business. My brother was also prone to anger and they may have felt they didn't want to work with an angry person. Like all family businesses it provided work for family members who weren't bright enough to support themselves by other means. One cousin left school with no qualifications and obtained work changing car tyres. He didn't succeed at that so found work in the shop!

The proudest moment in family life was when we bought a new car. The only perk of owning a shop was being able to buy a car 'on the firm.' In those days you visited the garage. Garages were oily rag places. The car showroom hadn't been invented. We always had Fords because their gears were so good! So off we went to the Ford garage. There was a choice of very few models. We usually had a consul. Once we had a Zephyr, which was very 'posh' but mainly it was a Consul. Once the model was selected there were only three options, the seats, bench or bucket, the colour, we always had beige, it didn't show the dirt, and the final choice was whether you had over riders on your bumpers. We always did because they were supposed to be safer. That was it. It took about half an hour at most. I remember one new car being delivered about a week before we went on holiday. The gears for which Fords were famous packed up when we were crossing the Alps. Pretty scary stuff.

It was the shop that allowed the family to stand up against the hostility of the world. It was the shop that made us feel good about ourselves. It was the shop that gave us our security in a world that was emerging from the deprivations of two World Wars.

When my Father died, we sang a hymn at his funeral, chosen by my Mother, which contained the line, 'but oh, my friend, my friend indeed, who at my need his life did spend.' It was the only moment in my entire life, where I was aware of feeling any emotion about my Father, because for the first time I realized what it was that Fathers do for their families. They spend their lives providing for their families. The families take this for granted and they receive no thanks. They just do it.

I imagine that most children are aware of their Father's love for them, but not me. That doesn't sound strange to me but it may do to you. How damaging is that to live your life not knowing love? Even if I had grown up in an orphanage there may have been some kind soul there who would have made the children feel loved and valued.

My Father didn't enjoy his life working amongst relatives he despised. He probably hated it; he was little more than a shop assistant, in the same shop for over fifty years. Selling saucepans and tin openers. His only companion, Joyce Merry, and she wasn't any fun I can tell you! I felt sad because he was gone and I hadn't had a moment's closeness. Not a moment in his entire life and yet he'd spent his life providing for me and the rest of his family. He must have felt love but he had never shown it and now I think about it neither had I, but that was because I had never felt it. Not for a moment. To spend your entire life feeling no love for either of your parents. They were like total strangers. I keep having to remind myself that I was the child in that relationship. It wasn't my fault I hadn't felt or shown love for my parents. They didn't notice that they had a son who showed them nothing but indifference and they wouldn't have cared even if they had. Little dick died from neglect but I am coming to find him and tell him it wasn't his fault.

My next job was working at weekends as a petrol pump attendant. In those days people expected to have the petrol put in for them. Before automatic cut-off nozzles it would have been dangerous not to. I often worked an evening shift and there was very little to do. I have to say that I loved this job. So much better than working in the shop. I worked entirely on my own but the customers were friendly. You would ask them if they wanted their oil and water checked and if there was time you could do their tyres which usually warranted a tip. One evening with nothing better to do I decided I would like to have ago at smoking. I bought 10 Senior Service, probably not a wise choice especially as they were untipped. I could never get the hang of it. This was in retrospect a huge blessing! Later in life

I tried smoking French cigarettes because I liked their smell but still couldn't manage it.

It was at the filling station that I met Dorothy and fell in love. She was working on the shift that followed me. She was so beautiful and I felt so lucky. I had a place at Cambridge, a girlfriend and a job, which gave me some money for the first time in my life. I could rely on my Mother to destroy this happiness.

I had always fainted from time to time and often without cause. My Mother decided that at the age of 18 I might be epileptic and sent me to the Doctors to arrange tests. I had just passed my driving test and was enjoying the freedom that brought, but she decided it wasn't safe for me to drive. As you can imagine, this made me extremely angry, but again I couldn't say anything. I resigned myself to doing what she commanded. It didn't take them long to decide there was nothing wrong with me but it was something to add to the list of things I could never forgive.

At the end of every shift we had to count the money and do a stock take, counting every can of oil, every light bulb and reading the meters on the petrol pump. The cash was put in a bag and the last person working in the evening locked up and took the bag to the Pub across the road who locked it in their safe over night. As far as I was concerned it was a foolproof system. You couldn't squeeze out even a pint of petrol. Every drop had to be accounted for. I didn't though have a criminal mind!

One morning the bag was collected from the Pub and one bag of cash was found to be missing. It could have been one of three attendants or someone at the Pub. I was interviewed by the Police but couldn't 'help them with their enquiries.' The Garage owner later told me that the main suspect was the girl in the shift before me whose best friend needed an abortion, which in those days cost about £50. It never occurred to me to count the number of money bags that I took to the Pub or I would have known one was missing.

The most bizarre episode at the Petrol Station was when Shell launched their 'Shell Make Money' campaign. With every visit you were given half a pretend bank note. If you could get two halves that fitted together you would be given the value of the note you had. It was sometimes £5 sometimes £10 and it was even possible to win £50. It was somebody's great idea but it sadly misfired. The forecourt was log jammed with motorists buying just half a gallon, getting their half note and driving round to the back of the queue to get another. Total chaos.

There was no 'plastic' in those days. All sales were cash. There was an occasional account customer but cheques weren't accepted at all. It amazed me seeing the huge wads of cash people carried about with them. I quickly and graphically learned about the "haves and the have nots.'

Today young people have to work their way through University. This was unheard of in my day. We were very lucky indeed to have Grants, which paid our way.

CHAPTER 8 NARCISSISM

I had a dream the other day. I was on a bus that was taking runners to the start of a race. When we arrived I found I had lost my bag and in it my running shoes and my phone. I was told that two 'white people' had stolen it. I looked and looked. I found the bag and one shoe but I knew that without the other shoe I would be unable to run. I was less worried about the phone although there were some numbers, which were irreplaceable. I would have to wait for them to phone me so I could explain. I never found the shoe.

I imagine we all grow up thinking our family is normal. We have no other way of knowing until we start a relationship with someone, meet their family and start comparing families, beliefs and values. We think our Mother is wonderful too. I grew up wishing and hoping that I'd been adopted. That one day my real family would find me and take me away. It was the only way I could explain to myself why I didn't feel loved and why my love was never returned. I could find no point of contact between me and my family. I later learned that this is a common feeling of children who have been abused, but at the time I just felt as if I was an alien in a foreign world. A world where nothing made sense. Like someone from the Church at the Chapel Christmas party. I didn't even look like them.

There was a boy in our village who had the same birthday as me and his father was a policeman. I wondered if he might have been my Father. But nobody came to take me away.

As a Father of four children I have had to invent being a Father. I had no idea of what Fathers do. It seems very natural to be genuinely amazed at your children's achievements. To say, 'well done,' 'that's wonderful.' Can you imagine the damage done by parents who never said things like that? You grow up assuming you are not a very good person. That you are a failure.

But how to work it all out? How do you unwrap fifty years of wishing you were dead? How do you discover the person you might have been? How do you find, 'little dick?' How do you rebuild the life that remained derelict? Why bother?

Strange how things happen in life. In 2005 there was a well-publicized case of a young man who killed his elderly parents. He left them in their bungalow, stole his Father's credit card and went off to America with his girl friend. He told her he was a professional tennis player and had signed a contract with a sponsor. She believed every word. She was in love with him and thought he was wonderful. He made sure she believed that by creating a fantasy world where he was at the centre and she fell for it totally. For the first time I heard the word, 'narcissist'.

A narcissist is a person with a personality disorder. Their personality is disordered which is to say, it is arranged in an unnatural, unhealthy, damaged way. They live in a fantasy world of their own creation.

They are at the centre and only see the world as a reflection of themselves. They are people who cannot accept their true selves, constructing instead a fixed mask that hides emotional numbness. Typically they have no feelings and cannot imagine what a feeling might be. They seek to control those around them and are more concerned with how they appear to others. To such an extent that they ignore anything that conflicts with their distorted idea of themselves. I discovered that my Mother was a fairly typical narcissist. For the first time I had a clue that it might not be all my fault.

She too lived in a fantasy world and the only feelings she had were feelings of anger when the world failed to match up with her idea of what it should be. She always finished your sentence for you. Whatever you were saying she always thought she knew what you were going to say. However fast you spoke she always managed to say your last word for you. It effectively stripped away your thoughts and ideas. She knew everything because she controlled her world.

She described the day my Father died as, 'the most wonderful day of my life'. She was always saying how much she loved him. They had been married for over fifty years and she didn't shed a tear. I remember the phone ringing that afternoon when I was at the office. It was a friend of my Mother's. The phone was handed to her. 'Your Daddy has died', she said. Now my Father had never, ever, in our family been referred to as 'Daddy'. But the use of that word put me in the position of a young child and her as the controlling parent. There was no expression of regret, just the telling of how it had happened. He had said he felt faint, she had gone to get him a glass of brandy and by the time she got back with it, he had gone. It was described as 'wonderful' because she had experienced 'the Lord' being with her throughout the day. The reality was that she had been the centre of attention throughout the day so her fantasy world was intact.

My brother once asked her why she hadn't shed a tear. She said simply, 'because I was free'. She was free to do what she wanted, to go where she wanted, to play the piano during the news, to eat when she wanted and to go to bed when she wanted. She had no idea, no feelings, that two boys had lost their Father, five grandchildren had lost their Grandfather, or that she had lost a companion of fifty years. She only saw this cataclysmic event as something that freed her to live unchallenged in her own world. To a narcissist this was a truly magnificent moment in her life.

A narcissist can't imagine how others feel. They can't imagine how they affect others. They aren't cruel or unkind, they just don't have the ability to put themselves in other peoples shoes.

My Brother once bought his wife a nice clock to go on the shelf above their fireplace. Nothing very expensive, just a nice clock. My Mother went out and bought herself the same clock to put on the shelf over her fireplace. It was a typical narcissistic act. She would never imagine how angry it would make my Brother and his wife. Her world had to conform to her fantasy; it had to have the sort of clock that her son would have bought for her. Even though he hadn't and wouldn't. She couldn't imagine him wanting to buy something for his wife and not for her. She couldn't imagine anyone having anything better than she had.

Here's another true story that was told to me by someone with a narcissistic Mother that illustrates the problem. This person had an abusive and violent Father who used to hit her for no reason. One day this happened and her Mother said, 'I wish you wouldn't make your Father angry, you must know how upset it makes me to see him hit you like that.' There was absolutely no understanding of how her daughter felt at being hit. Her world was entirely dominated by what she felt. There's no room in the parent child relationship for the child's feelings so the child grows up in the belief that her Mother's feelings are the only ones that matter. If her Mother is unhappy then it's her fault.

It has always interested me how rape victims and other victims of violence and abuse, very often blame themselves for the terrible thing that has happened. There is something cruelly called a 'victim mentality' but that is what happens to victims. You blame yourself. But it's not your fault. You didn't make it happen. It just did!!

Sadly, I've also encountered narcissism at work where it's just as dangerous and just as damaging.

I have a colleague who is totally driven to the point of obsession with taking over his business world.

This also includes my business world. It's not a long-term objective. He wants it all and he wants it now and he'll stab in the back anyone who gets in his way. He tries to be charming and believes he's well liked. In reality everyone loathes him. Everyone is terrified of him. With someone like that you can't penetrate their fantasy. You can't bring them down to earth. You can't tell them that they're a bastard. Nobody ever has, particularly their parents. Parents who think their child can do no wrong create narcissistic children, who believe them. Parents who give their children everything they want, create narcissistic children. In fact, we've created a narcissistic world where everyone expects to have exactly what they want, when they want it, which is usually now. Credit cards are the tools that create a narcissistic society. There's no room for kindness except as a means to persuade and manipulate. Nobody wants to be a social worker, nobody wants to be a teacher who can possibly do anything else. These are now the lowest regarded professions in our Society. Yet this has changed in a generation. My school was staffed by Oxbridge graduates. The cream of the academic crop. This wouldn't happen today.

Before the War the great psychological problem of Western society was anxiety and shame. Now it's depression. No one used to be depressed, they used to be repressed. People had massive sexual frustration and guilt. Most of that suppressed sexuality has now been lifted. We are now free to express our sexuality where and how we like. We're now depressed at the perceived inadequacy of our lives, our body shape, our failures, our inadequacies. Our inability to achieve what the media leads us to believe is our entitlement. We therefore have created for us, a fantasy world to measure ourselves by. And it's never as good as it should be. Never before have we had such expectations because never before has it been so easy to create a perfect world for ourselves. There's credit to buy things with and cosmetic surgery to mould the rest of it into shape! Who wants to be a schoolteacher a social worker, a nurse or indeed anyone who could make other people's lives better? No, we want to make our own lives better and we want it better, sooner rather than later. 'Now would do nicely, 'because I'm worth it!' For everything else there's MasterCard!

A real tragedy is that partners of narcissistic people get drawn into the fantasy world. They believe the lies; they believe that their partner is just wonderful. Basking in the glory of being in this world with this wonderful person no one tells them the truth. No one dares. They have affairs and their partners believe their lies. They are totally believable. In the business world the narcissist creates acolytes who feed the fantasy knowing they are backing a winner. They may be but the winner will stab them in the back if there's any slight advantage in doing so.

If I wanted I could paint you a picture of my Mother that's very different to the one you're reading. If you placed her at the centre and looked outward you would see a world that beat a path to her door, that hung on her every word, that looked to her for advice and inspiration. She was the Teacher, the world was her class, needing to learn from her. Needing to be good for her. She believed her pupils worshipped the ground she walked on.

My Mother was 'High Church' of England. More Catholic than the Catholics. She decreed that my Father's body would be placed in her Church overnight before the funeral. He would have hated that as he never went to Church, and hated going to the few weddings and funerals he was obliged to go to. It was like making him suffer even though he was dead! But then she could never have imagined any feelings apart from her own.

He was buried in the village Church yard. When the headstones appeared later that year we found that he had been buried alongside a man described as a 'Missionary and Preacher'. I thought this was a terrible fate for the old boy until I realized it was probably worse for his neighbour, condemned to an eternity of fruitless attempts to convert him to the religious way of life.

Of course he continued to fulfill a sort of role even in death. She talked to him constantly and of course he never disagreed or interrupted. She had her companion but none of the disadvantages of him making demands of her. She carried on having the same holidays at the same hotel at the same time of year and wasn't even inconvenienced by having to carry her own suitcase as she usually commandeered a passing stranger to fulfil that role.

She told the story of how she was walking along the beach and a gust of wind blew off her hat. It blew away down the beach too fast for her to catch it. 'Oh Richard,' she said/commanded, and the hat stopped dead long enough for her to retrieve it. Her power was awesome. She even commanded the spirits of the dead to obey her. Note that it was always, 'Richard'. Never 'Dick'. which he was to the rest of the world.

Names are important it seems to me, little dick.

My Mother had been 'Gladys' all her life. Not a great name, but her name. In middle age she decided she wasn't going to be 'Gladys' any longer and announced to the world that she was going to be 'Mary'. This totally confused people, particularly my Father who now didn't know who he was married to! He usually settled for 'Mother'. Couldn't go wrong with that. But when you think about it, always calling your partner 'Mother' simply creates a Parent/ Child relationship. It probably suited them both.

Now I don't want to give you the impression that my Mother was a bad person or an unlikable person. She was anything but. She had a large circle of very close friends. You had to see to believe the huge numbers of Christmas cards she received. Sadly, she needed to be adored. She worked very hard to make it so. She kept in touch with people in an incredible way. People all over the world. Relatives and people she had met on her travels. In the last years of her life when she was virtually housebound, she boasted that the world came to her as indeed it did. Her friends and next door neighbours waited on her, hand and foot in an amazingly unselfish way.

People enjoyed her company. The police lady who visited her for the routine visit necessary after a sudden, unexpected death like my Father's became a close personal friend and my Mother her confidante. It didn't stop her telling all and sundry this poor girls problems. Gossip gives people status and power. She was always ready to advise and counsel others. A cynic would say this was because she always knew best.

Beginning to understand my Mother's way of thinking was a great step forward but it was like finding one running shoe and not the other. It wasn't going to be enough on its own. And you needed friends. But a friend who never phoned was no friend. They were not worth clinging onto. No point mourning the loss of their number.

I wonder if the two 'white people' who had stolen my bag were my Parents. Running shoes are not that difficult to replace even though you miss the race. There are always other shoes, other races

CHAPTER 9 RELIGION

I badly needed a new map to take me through life now that I had lost my way. The old map had taken me down a cul de sac. Like driving the wrong way down a motorway, you're bound to crash and when you do, you have to find your way back to where you started so you can start again, this time heading in the right direction. The problem with motorways is that one direction is very much like another, and essentially they all look the same.

Because of my escape route to the church choir 3 or 4 times a week I was being fed a map and directions that were leading me away from where I now know I should have been going.

My young mind was very impressed by the dangers of being like the Pharisees. In the New Testament they stood for everything that Jesus was against. They were self righteous, arrogant and proud. They observed the letter of the law ignoring the spirit. I leaned that pride was the greatest danger of all. You just had to be terribly humble to stand a chance. If my Mother's treatment of me had left a few gaps then religion made the damage complete. I was desperate to be thought of as a good boy. So how do you become a good boy? In my Mother's world, good boys went to church, sang like angels and behaved in the way the Church taught. So, that's what I did. I never missed. Whenever Church was open I was there. I even went to choir practice so as to 'get it right.' My Mother never went with me. She went to another Church on her own. So there was me being good and she was never there to see it. No wonder I never felt cared for.

Having rejected all my family values, all the principles my parents stood for, I spent a lifetime trying to be a good Christian. You couldn't for a moment think you were OK. That could be rewarded with eternal damnation. No, at every turn you have to pray for forgiveness. Even now I will say many times a day the ancient 'Jesus' prayer, 'Lord Jesus Christ, Son of the Living God, have mercy on me, a sinner,'

It reinforced my reaction to my childhood influences that everything was somehow my fault. And when I say, 'everything,' I mean absolutely everything. Even the weather, if it spoils things I felt responsible for not making things better.

So, as a young choirboy I listened and listened and learned how to become like Jesus. I believed that if I worked at it, I might somehow make blind people see and the lame walk. Miracles start to happen if you stop believing in coincidences. It was all very easy.

So, by the time I was 16 I was an expert. In a school of 1000 pupils the headmaster asked for volunteers to organize help for the elderly and house bound. I was the only volunteer. This was the job for me. It was quite successful as I press ganged some others to trim old ladies hedges, run errands and generally behave in a saintly fashion. I somehow volunteered for meals on wheels and was extremely moved by the plight of elderly people. The meals were collected from an old Victorian Building, which had been the Leicester workhouse. It was a vile place and the smell was diabolical.

My Mother was very angry at all this 'do-gooding' as she called it. 'Charity begins at home' was thrust at me, I could never understand how a church-going person could have that attitude. But then she only saw the world as centering on her.

When I came to choose my A-level subjects RE was at the top of the list. I was good at it, as it had dominated my young life up to that point.

I was saddened that I had absolutely no belief in God, however hard I tried. Even when I had the experience floating about in the ambulance it only reinforced my view that there was no-one up there. Such was my isolation and loneliness I really couldn't believe that any celestial being could be interested in me and if he was, how come I was so unhappy, so unlovable, so desperate to find love and affection somewhere somehow.

Off I went to University to carry on the search for the Jesus of history. Cambridge was then if not now, at the forefront of modern Radical Theology. Even the greatest Theologians of the time had come to the conclusion that you just couldn't get even close. 'God' was an abstract concept, like peace or love and that was it. I once attended a lecture given by the then Regius Professor of New Testament Theology Dennis Nineham, who declared that in his considered opinion there was not a single word in the New Testament or indeed anywhere else that could be attributed to the Jesus of History. So I gave up the search and never went to Church again, not even at Christmas, until a very curious thing happened.

Twenty years on, I was in a bookshop when I came across a book by one of my old Cambridge Supervisors. It was Don Cupitt's, 'Sea of Faith'. There had been a T V Series and this was the book. I wrote to him to say how much I had enjoyed the book and did he remember me? Almost by return came a card with the postal frank over the stamp, 'Jesus Saves', and he said that not only did he remember me but would I like to attend a conference he was planning in my home County of Leicestershire? The Conference was a meeting together of people who were highly radical in their approach to religion to such an extent that none of them believed in an objective, 'out there' sort of God. Many were Vicars and Priests who could lose their parishes if their views had been made known.

A small group of us met again at Loughborough to work out a way forward and we agreed upon a form of words to describe what we were about, 'a network to explore the idea of religious faith as a human creation.' I was very enthusiastic about this as a movement to halt the decline in religion and suggested we add the word 'promote'. To this day the Networks motto is, 'to explore and promote the idea of religious faith as a human creation'. It has become a worldwide phenomenon with the name 'Sea of Faith,' and I am very proud of my involvement in getting it off the ground.

Did you notice the use of the words, 'very proud'? It took me a long, long time to be able to use that sort of language.

Most people were on their way out of organized religion. For me it worked the opposite way and I started to attend Church again and have done ever since. I have a very real awareness of something happening when I go. It helps me in a way I can't explain, and helps ease my feeling of worthlessness and loneliness. It's about being part of a caring community. I read the lesson and do it quite well.   Going to Church gives you an opportunity to think about things. It gives you ideas and helps to make sense of things. I listen to stories about Pharisees and I can see where I went wrong. If the world of Spirit is out there somewhere, where better to tell them what you think and need. Where better for them to tell you what you need to know.

When I think of the people that have had the greatest influence on me they are all clerics. There was 'Holy Joe' Ireson at School who was the first person to have believed in me. There was the Dean of Caius College Cambridge who was the second person to believe in me, and more than that, offered me friendship and a glimpse of what it would be like to be a truly good person. And lastly there was a strange Catholic Priest, Canon McBride.

Canon, or Father McBride was an amazing person. After my divorce I wanted to marry Helen, a

Catholic from a very Catholic family who would be devastated if their daughter married in a Register Office. I tried the Church of England but remarriage of divorcees wasn't possible in those days. I thought there was even less chance in the Catholic Church but Father McBride not only made it possible he welcomed me like a long lost friend. I felt truly, 'wanted'. This was very important to me. I was keen to return the favour in any way possible. Having married in the Church I toyed with the idea of becoming a Catholic as well.

I struck a deal with God. If God would bless us with children he could have me as a church going Catholic. He did and I have always stood by my side of the deal. I've been a Parish Councilor Clerk to the School Governors and always attended Mass come rain or shine. I've tried and failed to bring my children up as good Catholics. I'm now the only one that goes and as attendances decline I still cling to the rail like a passenger on the Titanic.

Religion had told me to be self-critical and deal with my inadequacies. It was the opposite of what I needed to hear and sent me the wrong way down the motorway of life. Now it helps me on my lonely journey. It gives me a street light on a dark road.

I know that I can find my way back and begin to dig up the body that was little dick. I can find that tiny house that's mine, and clear away the weeds that have grown up whilst I've been away.

So, there we have a chapter about the effect religion had on me and never once did I use the word, 'feeling' or 'felt.' What does that show?

Well, it shows how I have always had to 'think' my way through life. Most people experience life through their emotions. I can't. Those emotions were crushed, stifled, not deliberately, but inevitably for a boy brought up by a narcissistic Mother. This is why I have to rediscover little dick. This is why I have to rebuild the house. All that I have written here is about a boy desperate to feel loved. Trying as hard as he can to win approval. Others may react in different ways. Some may rebel, others may scream and shout to get noticed. I tried to an astonishing extent to be good. I would have done it for a living; I'd have become a Vicar if only I could have believed in God.

Let me share a 'feeling' with you. A feeling I have never shared with anyone before. It's both ridiculous and extremely sad. When the Queen announces her birthday honours list, or the New Years honours list, I'm always disappointed I don't get a mention! Yes! Really! I think I've been good and done so much for local charities. Something inside me is desperate to win approval from someone, anyone. Even the Queen! Lollypop ladies get mentioned; politicians get mentioned, but never me. Never the vast majority, I know. But........I would really like to know if anyone else feels that. I'm sure they do. Little dick always feels alone and it's never a comfort knowing others are worse off than you.

I'm the sort of person who volunteers for everything going. I can never say no, because to do so would be to risk disapproval. That would be too much to bear.

When I was first married we had some friends, Laurie and Sheila, who had a little girl, Rebecca, who was diagnosed as having a terminal liver disease. At the time there was no treatments, no transplants, no specialist units, no hope. None.

There was no Internet so even the scientists interested in the subject had great difficulty learning what others were doing. Laurie was a Graduate scientist who happened to be working as a market gardener. Sheila was a Nurse. Their hospital notes had him down as a Gardener with no employment record for Sheila. Laurie knew about genetics but the Doctors talked to him in childish terms thinking he wouldn't understand. With access to the Cambridge University Library we had found out everything there was to know in the world about liver disease in children. Laurie shared this with the Doctors who were suitably chastened especially when they realised he wasn't a 'gardener.' Jesus had the same problem in the Garden of Gethsemane. (If you don't know the connection you could try and read about it! It's in a very interesting book!)

There was no support group so Laurie and Sheila set about forming one. There was a family in Nottingham who had lost their son and the Father, Peter, had run the London Marathon to raise money for research. The Michael McGough Foundation for Research into Childhood Liver

Disease was founded and I was asked to help. Parents of children with liver disease were often reluctant to be involved such was the stigma of liver problems coming from the association with alcohol. The fund grew as did support. A research centre was established at Kings College Hospital. There was now some hope, somewhere to turn, and some treatments started to be discovered.

The fund was offered a half marathon being organised in Docklands as a fundraiser. It was just after Christmas and the race was at Easter. Laurie phoned me. He had to drum up a coach load of runners. Would I do it? Well, apart from cross-country at school I had never even run for a bus! I lie! I remember running to lectures at Cambridge. I enjoyed running rather than walking but never more than a few yards. I was working out at a Gym at the time and asked a fitness instructor if he thought I could get fit enough to run thirteen miles in the six weeks available. He said it wasn't possible but if I didn't mind running a bit and walking I'd get round….eventually.

I remember my first run. It was about half a mile. In plimsoles! I did it but was totally cream crackered! Only six weeks, I had to step it up, so the next day I did twice as much and felt terrible. Bit by bit I built up to a reasonable distance of about six miles. About half the distance I needed. I was on the coach going to London. There were a lot of 'hardened' runners!

Off we started and about half way round we were overtaken by the leading group headed by no less a runner than Emile Zatopek. An Olympic Champion! The speed he was going was astonishing. If you see it on the Telly you have absolutely no idea at the phenomenal pace those guys run at. Not only did I run all the way without stopping, inspired by my friend Emile I finished in quite a respectable time. And what did I think? What did I feel? I felt that it wasn't much of an achievement and I'd better have a go at a longer distance. Being me, you never have any feeling of satisfaction, just feelings of failure and inadequacy, tried hard but could do better.

I was sitting in a Sauna at the Gym and was talking to a friend. Phillip. He'd completed a marathon and I thought to myself, 'well if he can so can I.' I entered the Ipswich Marathon and trained hard for it.

It was a hard slog and about half way round my knee started to hurt, rather badly. At the end I was in agony although I'd done quite a good time. Where were the feelings now? I only felt failure that my knee had let me down. I had to try again. Two days after the race I thought I'd go for a run but only just made it down the road before my knee gave out. It took months before I could run again.

I entered the Birmingham Marathon. I finished that in about 3 hours 35 minutes. A good time by anyone's standards, but yet again I felt I could do better. I had walked part of the way having been befriended by a guy who was a Military Policeman in Northern Ireland and very interesting too. If only I could run a marathon and run every step of the way. That would be in London and run I did, every step of the way, but yet again not as good a time as I'd hoped and not even as good as Birmingham.

On and on it went. Nine marathons and countless half marathons and 10K's. Never once did I have the feeling that I'd done well. And my Mother? When I ran London she watched on the television and was always quite certain she had seen me, almost impossible with the masses of people running. She always knew better, running would damage my knees and give me Arthritis just like her. Many years after she died a Doctor told me that there was no truth in this at all and my knee problems had nothing to do with Arthritis. She told her friends about 'our Steve' running the marathon but she never managed to say 'well done,' that would've been too hard.

The Michael McGough fund became the charity now know as 'Child' and the McGough family resigned in disgust. It had been 'their' thing. Their son's picture had been the logo but experts said that the picture of a dead child wasn't a good image to project. The Sun newspaper got on the band wagon with its 'tiddlers' campaign where readers sent in unwanted coins. There are now successful liver transplants and I'm glad I was involved in the beginning.

My next venture into charitable works was with Asbah the charity that helps people with spina bifida and hydro cephalus. A local saint, Meg Garnett was the local organiser and asked me to help. I couldn't say 'no.' It was an amazing experience meeting the heroic parents and their wonderful children. The local branch met for a number of years but eventually disbanded for the very best of reasons. Children with spina bifida didn't want to be regarded as a group, they were individuals first and their handicap, if handicap it was, didn't warrant them being treated as in any way special. I always took Harriet to the meetings and was glad she was able to see others who were different to her. How rare is that in a world where everyone seems perfect?

And how did I feel? I was doing my best, trying to be good and kind. Trying to win approval from people. Hoping to feel better about myself. Trying to achieve things. Trying to help. It's what Jesus taught after all, to love one another. But nothing worked, and I still run marathons. I still can't say 'no.' The whole enterprise is exhausting. I spend long hours at Trustee meetings, with people who talk but never turn up to fundraising events. Who always have ideas for things others can do, but never do anything themselves. I am Deputy Chairman of East Suffolk Mind but if you asked service users at the local Psychiatric Hospital if they had ever heard of it hardly any would. To be able to use its' services you have to be referred by the Governmental bodies who fund it. It's not enough to be in a state of mental distress you need to be assessed, processed approved and eventually allowed in. When they are closing hospital beds they have to be seen to be offering services to service users to keep them off the streets and it's certainly better than nothing. You get the feeling though that the service exists for the benefit of the people who run it first and the service users a poor second.

One great thing the East Suffolk Mind did was to set up the East Suffolk Advocacy Network. Working at the 'coal face' of mental health services it offers a voice to those who have none.

I would like at this point to share with you the story of Islay Moore. It shows the terrible shortcomings of the mental health services of this country and how far I went in my quest to become a 20th Century Saint.

In my professional capacity as a Solicitor I was asked to act for Islay, a lady of indeterminate age who wanted to sell the flat in which she lived. From the price she'd agreed I knew that she was being 'ripped off.' I met her in my office and she was clearly a very strange lady. She reminded me of the old lady, Tar Oil Lil, who visited my Father's shop from time to time. I patiently tried to piece together her story. It took me many months, she was such a disturbed person.

Islay was a schizophrenic. Her Mother who had bought the flat for her had supported her. Other money had been put in a Trust Fun after her Mother's death. She lived on her own for many years and wasn't any trouble to herself or the Community. She formed a relationship with Justin who was much younger than her and they were mutually supportive. Justin was OCD, a sufferer of an obsessive compulsive disorder, and he was really anxious about dirt and contamination. Islay received her medication from the Hospital but a new Consultant Psychiatrist decided she wasn't ill after all and took her off medication. She rapidly sank into the crazy world of schizophrenia. Justin had to leave her for the sake of what little sanity he had left. Islay's behaviour became seriously extreme and antisocial. Her flat was disgusting and totally uninhabitable. The toilet sink and shower were all blocked and the flat was knee deep in the sort of filth you would usually find in a municipal refuse dump.

I managed to gain access to the Trust Fund money so I could sort out the flat if only I could get her out of it long enough for builders to go in, gut it and rebuild it. Would East Suffolk Mind help? They did what they could, she could have a wash, get warm for a time and have something to eat, but short term accommodation? Not likely. She had to be nominated by Health and Social Services. I found a bed and breakfast place that would take her in for a few days and they deserve a medal for doing so. They accepted my personal guarantee that she wouldn't be violent and that they'd be paid. Here was a woman who was sometimes found lying naked in the gutter. She was vile and smelly and very frightening in her manner.

The builders did a phenomenal job in about three days and Islay returned home well pleased with her new accommodation.

Islay's flat was on the ground floor of a building with another two storey maisonette above. This had been vacant for some time no doubt because Islay was downstairs and eventually a 'For Sale' sign appeared. It was being repossessed. I knew nobody would buy it and waited several months before making a ridiculous offer to buy it. The mortgage company accepted so dipping into the Trust Fund Islay bought it. She moved in upstairs and reunited with Justin, he moved in downstairs. I completed the investment by buying the freehold for next to nothing so Islay now owned a valuably Town Centre property investment and was as happy as could be. She filled the flat with guinea pigs and a pet rat which gave her much enjoyment and company.

After a few years she and Justin decided they wanted to go to live by the sea in Wales which is exactly what they did. They lived happily ever after until Islay died from cancer just after Christmas 2006.

I saved Islay and Justin from all the governmental agencies, which at considerable expense had only served to destroy their lives. It shouldn't be forgotten that her behaviour had been unacceptably anti social although not her fault. Well done the boy Jesus!

CHAPTER 10 TRAVERS SMITH

As I sat on Peter's bed in Fulbourne Hospital Cambridge I had my first encounter with the black dog of mental illness that haunts so many of us. He really was no different from the Peter I knew, but the Peter I knew, wasn't the Peter of dark nights and even darker days. Drinking himself silly, a slave to the whirling pit. Staring at his bedroom light to try to stop the room spinning round. His landlady thought he was working late into the night. Little did she know. Little did any of us know.

Peter once told me that I was like a clear mountain stream. When you looked into it you could see straight through. There was nothing hidden. I must have seemed like that to him, as he was a person where so much was hidden. Where the mind had such dark impenetrable secrets. I took it as a compliment but others might have seen it as a criticism.

He told me that when he was a young boy he overheard his Mother on the phone to a friend saying that Peter was a 'mistake,' that he was the result of an unplanned and unwanted pregnancy. It was a devastating thing to have heard and it literally drove him mad with sadness, leading to desperate depression. He tried all his life to prove to his Mother that he was worthwhile but as a result, he couldn't bear the thought of failure. At the age of 11 he was marked out as a potential Oxbridge scholar and was always way ahead of others in his age group. When he took his O-Levels he tried to give himself food poisoning by keeping some cake in his wardrobe and eating it when it got mouldy. He failed to poison himself but passed the exams with flying colours. When it came to take his A-levels he stabbed himself in the hand so he couldn't hold a pen. This failed too as the school provided a writer to dictate to.

His parents kept a shop on a Council estate in Leicester and had no reason to expect him to do well. But whatever the reason, he couldn't stand the feeling of being unwanted and unloved and depression was his escape. I suppose I was lucky that nobody expected anything of me but that created a different problem, a chasm of self doubt that was just as hard to escape from.

He eventually left Cambridge and found gainful employment teaching English to prisoners at the Gartree High Security prison in Leicestershire. I later learned that he had risen through the ranks of the Civil Service to the lofty position of personal secretary to the Home Secretary.

On leaving Cambridge I became a trainee solicitor at a distinguished legal practice in the City of London, Throgmorton Avenue no less, with Travers Smith, Braithwaite. They were the only Solicitors in the Country not to have the word 'Solicitors' on their notepaper, 'if they don't know we're Solicitors they're not worth knowing.' They also didn't record the degrees of the Partners on their notepaper. They were all either 'Cantabs' or 'Oxons' (Cambridge or Oxford) so I suppose the same principle applied.

My interview with them was not unlike the one I'd had with Dick Gooderson at Cambridge. 'So you come from Leicester....would you know Alderman Sir Mark Henig?' My interviewer, John Humphries was at the time a member of the British Waterways Board, which was chaired by Mark Henig, then also Chairman of The English Tourist Board. 'Oh yes.' I said, 'he's a friend of my Father's, they were at school together.' That was probably enough to get me in. Little did they know that Sir Mark used to come into my Dad's shop and I was introduced on one such occasion. He wasn't exactly a 'friend.'

Unknown to me at the time, one of Tracers Smith's distinguished clients was the Guinness family and also the Brewery. The Senior Partner, William Wilberforce, 'Willy,' was on the board of the Brewery Company. The Baron Fairhaven was a member of the Guinness family and his family name was Broughton. When he wasn't being a Baron he was Sir Evelyn Delves Broughton. I imagine they must have thought I was a relation, but knowing Sir Mark was icing on the cake. It's not who you are, it's not what you are. It's who you know that's important.

As he showed me to the lift after the interview he asked me if I wanted to join them, I mentioned that I had another interview with Richards Butler who he dismissed with a, 'you don't want to join them, you ought to join us.' After that I didn't feel I had much choice!

John Humphries' secretary later told me that they didn't usually take on trainees before they had passed their Law Finals and I was an exception. It reinforced the feeling I'd had throughout life that everything that happened to me, getting to Wyggeston, getting to Cambridge and now getting into the City was a great, monumental mistake and that one day I would be found out and sent back to Leicester to be a Building Society manager! Should I have trusted my instincts or was my self image so poor that I couldn't appreciate that I was worthy of the success I had? What would little dick have done? Where would he have gone? He would have probably stayed in the City and been a resounding success and I'd be retired by now!

I once had the most bizarre conversation with the Baron Fairhaven. My phone rang, 'I'm Lord Broughton and I want to speak to Mr. Humphries.' 'I'm sorry; you've been put through to the wrong extension, because my name is Broughton.' 'No it isn't,' he said, 'my name's Broughton.' And we had one of those, 'no my name's Broughton,' conversations. It only confirmed my opinion and my family's opinion of the British Aristocracy. No wonder we had two World Wars!

Mr. Wilberforce wasn't a lot better but at least he was a kind, unpretentious man. The grandson of Lord Wilberforce the anti-slavery abolitionist. Willy was in the Army and fought in Burma. As did 'Jim'. Jim was a little wizened man who looked after our file store. His surname may have been Smithies but as his brother's surname was Smithers, he wasn't entirely sure. You would often find Jim and Willy sitting in the file store sharing a mug of tea chatting like old soldiers do.

Willy was also on the Board of Gratton Warehouses the catalogue and retailing company. Willy ran a catalogue and I shall never forget seeing him and Carol our delightful switch board operator leafing through the Gratton catalogue with Willy taking her order. Things are very different in legal practices today!

John Humphries told a story about Willy, which may or not have been true. Willy lived in Essex and commuted from Chelmsford Station. Now Willy's eyesight wasn't that good and he leaned out of the window of his compartment as the train just wasn't moving off and he was getting late. He saw someone in uniform standing on the platform and enquired, 'why isn't this train going?' 'I don't know,' came the answer. Getting frustrated he said, 'well why don't you know, you work for the railway don't you?' 'As a matter of fact I don't,' came the polite rely. 'Well who the fuck are you then?' said Willy getting very impatient. 'If you must know I'm the fucking Bishop of Chelmsford!!' came the reply, and indeed it was!

I suppose that if Mr Wilberforce could get by in life being 'Willy,' I could have survived being little Dick or even Steve.

On my first day at Travers Smith, John Humphries, the Partner I was attached to, asked me what they should call me. I couldn't bring myself to say 'Steve' which after all was what I was called, so instead, I told him my name was 'Stephen' being slightly more dignified and respectable or so I thought. So 'Stephen' stuck and I hated it. Even now I can't bring myself to tell people I'm 'Steve.' Starting as Richard then being Dick then Steve then Stephen. I'm now on my fourth name. My Mother liked calling me Francis, my middle name, just to complicate things further. If someone gives you a pet name, it's like ownership. With someone you love it's quite nice as the pages of messages in the Times on Valentine's day just go to show. From my Mother it was something I could have done without.

Curiously, although he was known as John, Mr. Humphries' real name was Anthony Charles. Maybe he had a mad mother too.

So, 'Stephen,' I now was. I was placed in an office with a quite Senior Partner called Adam Ridley. He was a very kind man and treated me with a touching respect. He was a man who loved the detail. I wasn't! One day he came in, sat at his desk, opened his newspaper, and burst into tears sobbing uncontrollably. All I could hear him say between sobs was, 'we've run out of bread'. I suppose it was the last straw. Margaret, our tea lady tried to enter the room to bring our tea but I managed a, 'not now Margaret' and somehow managed to get a taxi to take him home. I never saw him again. He occasionally phoned up from the home he'd been sent to asking me to send him files. I was told not to. I couldn't see that it would have done him any harm. He too was a singer, a close friend of Sir David Wilcocks the world famous conductor and composer. Adam had one of the first 'speaker' phones and I was therefore always able to hear the conversations that went on. It was a great education whilst it lasted. Adam's wife was an 'Honourable' and nearly all the clientele were 'gentry' public school, moneyed, people I could never have related to. I once saw a list of assets belonging to a young Scottish Earl. There were pages and pages, oil tankers, factories, villages, farms. Just unbelievable. Must have been quite a burden.

It was my second experience of a mental breakdown and taught me that however bad, nothing really mattered that much. A hard belief to stick to.

John Humphries asked me if I thought I could cope with Adam's work 'for the time being' and always a person to say 'yes' to any question there I was with about 18 months introduction to Law, in charge of a caseload of a Senior Partner. It seemed to work out OK with the help of the secretaries, who, like nurses in a Hospital always knew as much as you needed to know to get by.

I remember being asked to act for Willy's brother Lord Wiberforce, by then an Appeal Court Judge. He was buying a flat and I was to act for him. Is that scary or what?! Like a junior nurse being asked to take out the gall bladder of a Consultant Surgeon!

To get by in any walk of life you need to master what can only be called, 'bullshit.' More politely put you have to bluff your way through life. So bluff my way through acting for Lord Wilberforce I did. He was, like his brother, an extremely kind and gentle person. He said he didn't know anything about leases and if I thought the lease of his flat was OK then that was good enough for him! Phew, what a relief!

The City was very like Cambridge, all old buildings and 'jolly nice' people. Business people had the tradition of trusting each other's word. Nothing was written down, nobody would go back on their word even if they couldn't remember saying it. It was a training which led me to total disaster later in life at a time when the world had changed into a place where you trust no-one. Where given half a chance your best friend will stab you in the back whether or not it's to his advantage.

My time with Travers Smith was very good but I always felt that I was an impostor. An alien on the wrong planet so eventually I left even though I had been offered a partnership. I was at heart, little dick, a shopkeeper's son from Leicester. Not public school, not married to an 'honourable', not much really.

I think I would have been a good sheep farmer. I do love animals. My Uncle Bob told me that sheep were always having problems with their feet. That was a reasonable response. If your son has a dream like that like boys do, the natural reaction would be something to the effect, 'that would be nice' to enter into the dream, to validate his ideas. To tell him that his dream would make his Mother unhappy is to take away that dream. To deny that child his everyday dreams and visions of the future.

I was once on holiday in Devon, more sheep than people I don't doubt. The sheep were lovely, so lovely that I thought I should become a vegetarian. It then occurred to me that if the world stopped eating sheep then the fields and hillsides of Devon would be empty. I decided not to become a vegetarian. Each day on that holiday I went for a run along the cliff tops. One day I was sitting having a breather and I somehow received a 'message' in my mind that if I came to that place three days in a row, then on the third day I would receive another message. So, for three days, I ran to the same point and waited for the 'message.' I closed my eyes. There wasn't a soul to be seen and suddenly there was this voice as clear as anything, 'do you know the way down?' I opened my eyes to see an anoracked, bespectacled, male hiker. Probably not a supernatural messenger! I told him that I didn't know the way down. Neither did I know the way up, or any way at all for that matter. Many years later I lay at the bottom of another cliff, on the beach, not knowing the way down or the way up, or any way for that matter. So maybe it was a message after all.

On balance I think Uncle Bob was right. Sheep have terrible problems with their feet. I was better off as a Solicitor.

I have never been comfortable in male company. Since leaving my village school and my friend Rosemary, I've always sought female company. Wyggeston was all boys, Cambridge nearly all male. Office life was better. I've had many wonderful friendships with secretaries and female solicitors and paralegals. Later in life I joined the Round Table in an attempt to understand the bloke thing. It didn't work. They only want to talk about work port and cars. Maybe it was because I had no relationship with my Father.

In the Round Table I took charge of spending the money raised during the year. It had usually gone to Children's charities but I set about trying to find out where on a local level it was most needed. I quickly discovered that Mental Health was a Cinderella sector with meager resources and where a little money could go a long way.

I had written to the local Psychiatric Hospital, St Clement's, and had a most wonderful letter from an amazing man called Ray Barton. He was in charge of a ward known as 'Linkways' and its function was to prepare people for discharge. With Ray's guidance I helped introduce a whole series of events aimed at making the little money we raised go a long way. I was in Jesus mode! We took patients shopping, to the football, to the cinema and at Christmas we closed the Ward and took the entire Linkways community to Felixstowe for a Christmas tea. Some of the patients hadn't been out of the hospital for years but they all behaved impeccably to the astonishment of the staff who could hardly believe it.

The people I met there were so honest and open about their illness. They had no pretence and no embarrassment. There was however always the danger of suicide and many were still on 'sections'.

I remember once taking a delightful young man to a classical music concert. His Father was an architect and he had played the cello in an orchestra. I really enjoyed his company. At the interval we shared a beer together and he explained to me that his main problem in life was the IRA. They drove BMW's and when he was walking down the street he was worried that they would drive onto the pavement and run him down. It was so real to him. It showed me that we all have our own version of reality. Mine is different to yours, as yours is to mine. We can't judge how each other behave or react to the world we find ourselves in. His world was at times very frightening as was mine to become many years later.

One day at the office I met Ian Hartley, a former teacher and psychiatric patient who was starting East Suffolk Mind, a local mental health charity. I was eager to help in any way I could and became one of the first Trustees. I am now the longest serving Trustee and Deputy Chairman. Through East Suffolk Mind I helped start the East Suffolk Advocacy Network. I have also helped national Mind. It has been a wonderful part of my journey and brought me in touch with some very special people. Our local psychiatric hospital is a dark Victorian place and I remember talking to Gillian, a former patient who was starting the Advocacy network with us. I said how I thought it was such a terribly depressing place. She said that to her and many others it was the most wonderful oasis in a terrifying world. Her reality was her reality. Very different to mine.

One man I will never forget was known simply as Fred. He was nearly 70 when I met him as a patient in our local Psychiatric Hospital. He wanted to make his Will. The staff told me he had spent at least the last 40 years there unable to speak. Not a word. About a year previously he wad been 'adopted' by a young occupational therapist. She had taught him to paint and he taught himself to play the electric organ. Eventually he started to talk again.

Fred was very chatty and frank about his condition. He went into hospital for a routine operation on his stomach and when he awoke from the anesthetic he had lost the power of speech. The hospitals didn't know what to do with him. They thought the problem was 'all in the mind.' So, he went to the Psychiatric unit at the Hospital and was never released. He didn't seem to mind much, but then he was totally institutionalized and 'outside' was quite a frightening place. He once went to the opticians and the only other time he went out, he went to a concert given by a local organist. This had inspired him with his keyboard.

Fred told me how the nurses would steal from him in the night when they thought he was asleep. He was pretty angry about that. Such is the way psychiatric patients are treated.

He died shortly after and left his organ to the girl who had been so kind to him. Others leave other organs I know! I shall never forget Fred. It was a privilege to have known him.

For me Fred symbolizes the plight of the mentally ill in our Society. They have no voice. If they had a voice would anyone listen? They are sometimes looked after but who in Fred's lifetime thought about why he was the way he was and what could make him better? He wasn't a lot of trouble so he was looked after, sort of, and ignored. For a lifetime. All it took to unlock his illness, if illness it was, was a little kindness, a little interest from a caring person. And why did he have to wait a lifetime to receive it? What a terrible waste of a life and all the resources that made sure he would never be any better.

I believe Fred should be remembered and if this is part of that then this will have been worthwhile. He should have a memorial like we remember those who died in the two world wars. There are many like Fred and they should never be forgotten.

Jesus said that we should become like children if we wanted to enter the Kingdom of Heaven. It's an idea that you find in other Eastern Religions. It's about the simplicity and trusting nature of a child. It seems to me that those who have experienced mental illness are closer to the Kingdom of Heaven than any of us. Fred certainly was. They are people who have asked themselves the question, 'what's it all about, what's the point, why bother?' They may not have found the answer but at least they have learned enough to carry on. To get up in the morning and face another day. Even if it means taking a pill, or many pills.

Peter came through the darkness of depression. Many don't survive. But my psychic medium had told me that suicides are sent back to learn the lessons they thought they had escaped from. When life becomes too much I think about having to go through it all again. I could never contemplate the prospect. To this day it seems to me to be the biggest argument, perhaps the only argument, against committing suicide.

My Mother once said, 'the Lord never gives anyone a cross to bear that's too heavy.' But then she never knew anyone who suffered from mental illness. She never visited a psychiatric hospital. She probably wouldn't have been able to empathize even if she had.

I learned eventually to reprogram the tape recorder in the mind that said, 'I wish I was dead,' and instead it says, 'I want to be a Grandad one day.' And I think back to that lovely man who used to visit us, bringing a penguin biscuit as a treat, teaching me how to box, prize fighter style, that big gentle giant, that man my Mother loved so much, that man from Kettering where it all began. My Grandad, who was so brave. When a thief pointed a gun at him in his shop he grabbed the gun and the man ran away. He never recovered from the shock of that attack and I lost my Grandfather far too soon. And that made my Mother so angry. All I wanted was for her to be happy but she never was. Neither was I, but then, that had never mattered. The bastards killed my dog and never said sorry. Never explained why.

CHAPTER 11 ANGELS

It was a beautiful sunny day and for the first time ever I'd agreed to visit a client at her home. I shall never know what persuaded me to do that, but agree I did and at the appointed time I set off to my car. At the entrance to the car park was sitting a young man I recognized. On a bench. Under a tree. He was a locally well-known Radio Presenter. I nodded the usual salutation of recognition but for some reason I shall never know I decided to sit down beside him, even though I had little time before my appointment. We chatted a little and agreed that it would be good to meet up again for lunch, one day.

Some time later he was to tell me that he was sitting there trying to find the courage to call on the Samaritans whose office was opposite the bench. He'd had his eyes closed and was praying to God to send him an Angel to save him. He opened his eyes and there I was.

We met several times after that and he told me that he wanted to end his life. I said in all honesty that I thought this was an option for all of us. Was there any good reason you could give anyone not to? He felt liberated by this because he knew that anyone else, particularly his family would react in horror. But for him it was his best option. His life was a total success. He had a wonderful girl friend, now a popular TV presenter, a great career ahead of him. A great car and a loving family. But none of it seemed real. None of it seemed like it belonged to him. He was much like Peter. Talented, successful but with a life made hell by depression.

He recovered and is now working for the BBC in London.

I began to think that somehow I was part of God's plan. I was needed to do God's work. I thought back to the time in the Ambulance. Whatever plans I had, there were other plans and I had to survive to help out. How deluded can you be? I was still down the wrong road, travelling in the wrong direction. Looking for love, looking for affirmation of my worth, trying to be like Jesus. Thinking I was like Jesus, helping poor people stranded by life's roadside. I hadn't yet realized that I would never find that love. The love I'd been looking for had been denied me as a child and I'd never find it from anywhere else. I still hadn't found my running shoe. No one had said, 'sorry about your dog,' And I hadn't begun to find that tiny derelict house.

There were so many signs pointing in the wrong direction.

I mentioned being in the Round Table and one curious day I was approached by a young employee of the Forestry Commission who wanted some money to build a hard surfaced track in the forest in Suffolk to allow access for people in wheel chairs. It would have been the first of its kind in the Country. It was a brilliant idea. Except for the fact that it would take all our fundraising for about 5 years to gather the money.

Bob Geldoff had performed the miracle of Live Aid so I thought I would try a miracle of my own. And I did. Within a few months it had been built and was opened by Sir Leonard Cheshire the hero of Fighter Command and the founder of the Cheshire Homes for war veterans and disabled people.

The miracle didn't end there. The 'hurricane' of 1987 reduced the forest in Suffolk to flattened matchwood. All that is except the small part where the track had been created, and within a few hours it was back in action. It has now been extended and still serves the disabled community well.

Little dick. Miracle worker. But still as unhappy as ever. Still wishing I was dead. Still no closer to unraveling the mystery.

BBC Radio Suffolk opened in Suffolk in about 1990 and one of its main editors was Angela for whom I'd acted as solicitor when she moved to Suffolk. We had lunch and we talked about the new station. I told her that I thought that 'Thought For The Day' was possibly the worst program with a succession of Vicars going on about 'God, Jesus and the Bible.' In my Sea of Faith mode I was passionate about presenting religious ideas using non-religious language. She asked me if I would 'have a go,' and I agreed. I was to be the first ever non-vicar to present it and I became quite popular with the Radio Station and their audience.

One of my sayings is that you learn more from life's bad experiences than you do from the good ones. You certainly remember them more.

The first bad experience was the divorce. I'd rebuilt my home, my life, my family. The next bad experience was losing my job. It doesn't happen to solicitors. Partners in respectable established firms don't get the sack, but one day I was pressured into signing a Partnership Agreement and a year or so later a clause in that Agreement was used to get me out. Not with a months notice, or a month's pay in lieu of notice, but one day I was in and the next I was out.

It was totally devastating. I had huge outgoings with four children and two wives to support. No savings, no income. I couldn't put petrol in the car. I couldn't go to Sainsbury's. I couldn't buy a newspaper.

My youngest daughter broke her arm at about the same time so I was of some use looking after her. I thought that I must be being punished for some sin I had committed and there must have been plenty of those.

When I wrote the first draft of this book I ended this part of the story here and moved on to the next chapter. That in itself, tells a great deal about me, who I was, and how I reacted to things. My life was in ruins. I was totally desperate. Where were the feelings? Where was the anger, the fury? How do you write about emptiness? How do you write of being numb? The answer is that you don't. You move on to the next chapter. But this won't do. I have to relive my life, go back down the motorway and look at it from the other direction. Going back. It's all part of finding the house, finding little dick and putting it all together and it isn't easy. Trying to feel feelings you never had, or if you had them, you felt they were of no value because no one cared.

It all came about because of a mistake by a colleague, which I should have confronted better than I did. In my business world the mortgage lenders are all powerful and when the mistake was discovered the mortgage lender decided to suspend my practice from their panel of approved legal advisers. This any of them can do, at any time, giving no reason and with no right of appeal. It effectively destroys your business, your livelihood and most importantly, your reputation. When you're being entrusted with huge sums of money and trusted to give important advice, reputation and credibility are paramount. Without it you're history.

The senior partner was a man I despised totally. He wasn't bright, had no education, did very little work and essentially lived off the backs of people like me. He was 'public school,' something I could never abide. The arrogance of them all. These were the people who had led the country to two world wars. And yes, I was probably jealous. Jealous of their wealth. Jealous of their privileged lifestyles. He came to my room at about 5pm that afternoon and told me I'd been suspended by the partners, my partners, and that I would be hearing from them. That was the last conversation I had with any of them. And the last time I set foot in the office. The work and investment of time energy money, and yes, even love I'd put in over more that 20 years was gone. I was out. Down and out. I couldn't believe that anyone would treat another person this way. Someone who had given loyal service. In the end it all counts for nothing.

I trudged my weary way home not knowing what on earth to do. That is, apart from making an appointment with a doctor for a prescription for Seroxat. I knew I would need help to deal with this mentally. Seroxat would dull the pain. It would make you feel like shit for about 2 weeks, make you feel worse, but if you survive that, it should make you feel able to cope in the long run. Just having the tablets in a cupboard makes you feel a little less defenseless.

The next Saturday morning the postman rang the doorbell with a recorded delivery letter. I now have real problems coping with Saturday mornings. I'm better when the postman has been and gone. If the postman rings the bell it's terrible. It brings it all back. I can't remember what the letter said, even at the time everything was like a terrible dream, but the letter confirmed I was dead and buried.

Anyone else would be angry. I just wished I was dead. That's the only way I could deal with things. The anger I should have felt became just emptiness, nothing. I was facing losing my family, my home and never being able to work again. No one wants a disgraced solicitor. There's no going back and starting again. You're bad news.

In a few days it would be my youngest daughter's birthday. I remember the parents bringing her school friends to our house for her birthday party. There were all these rich and powerful people with their big cars and no money worries. There was me with no money to put petrol in my car!

I remember phoning my Mother to tell her what had happened. She was living alone virtually housebound with Arthritis. I knew I would soon be homeless. I had lost my family and the means of supporting them. I offered to return home and look after her. How crazy was that! But when you're desperate you have some crazy ideas. She wouldn't hear of it. Didn't say, 'come and talk about it.' She wasn't interested in my failures only my success. It summed up our relationship. There was no discussion of what my feelings might have been, or what she could do for me. No wonder I felt worthless. The most important person in the world didn't care, didn't offer any help, wasn't concerned so there was no point in having feelings, to expressing your feelings, to expecting any one to care.

A friend who had worked in legal practices all her life, Sue, had once worked at the most prestigious legal practice in the country, Theodore Goddard. She was friendly to another secretary there who had married one of the solicitors, a guy called Pietro, who specialized in these sort of things. He agreed to see me as a favour to Sue even though I had no way of paying him. I set out to walk to the railway station on my way to my appointment to see him in London. I called at a cash point on the way to see if I had any money in the bank. I didn't, skint. Thank God for credit cards. I could buy a train ticket even though I would never be able to pay for it.

Theodore Goddard have very impressive offices in the City. The firm was founded by Mr. Goddard a sole practitioner and they were now top people. London lawyers have it fairly easy, they just get into a taxi and take their clients' problems to specialist barristers so off we went to see one. I think he must have agreed to do it for free as well.

My former partners had no idea what was about to hit them. You can't imagine what it is to be a provincial lawyer up against the big boys. It's like getting into the ring with Joe Frazier. It was very satisfying knowing I could fight back. They needed me to resign from the partnership so they could tell the mortgage lender they'd dealt with the problem. If someone wants something from you, you have a degree of control. But what did I want from them? I would have begged them for any sort of job, I'd have made the tea, done the photocopying, any thing. But it wasn't to be. A clause in the partnership agreement prevented me from working for any one else. If they agreed to lift that I had a slim chance of surviving. They knew that if they agreed I could take away a large chunk of their work and they would give to someone else the person who had built up their firm to where it was today.

They had no choice but to agree so the deal was done.

Days passed. Weeks passed. I had an idea to make contact with a local solicitor I knew who had set up on his own. He agreed to take me on despite the fact that I was 'damaged goods,' and the rest is now history. We created within 10 years a firm with a £3 million turnover. One of the top 500 firms in the country, the 2nd biggest firm of residential conveyancers in the eastern region and the 5th largest in the country. The firm who ditched me struggled on but to my enormous satisfaction never really recovered from my departure.

So, I'd rebuilt my personal life and rebuilt my professional life but still no sign of little dick. The house was still derelict. Still no sign of my other shoe!

I have what I call 'broughton's law of opposites.' It seemed to me that people act in the opposite way in which they should to achieve the result they want. People in relationships want to be loved but the way they behave makes loving them well nigh impossible. So it occurred to me that if you want to get it right you have to react in the opposite way to the way you would instinctively. If you're accused unjustly you would normally react in a hostile manner which will only serve to reinforce the accusation you are facing. Positions become entrenched and there's no way out. If you admit you are wrong even though you don't feel it you immediately diffuse the situation and as often as not you are met with a conciliatory response which allows all pride to be retained.

I now feel that this isn't as good as I thought it was! It's a product of a person afraid to express his feelings, afraid of confrontation, afraid of emotion.

CHAPTER 12 JONATHAN and JOAN

I once heard a story used to illustrate how the mental health services of this Country operate. It was told by a Professor of Psychiatry from Cambridge. It's the story of the camel castrator.

The camel castrator explained how he castrates camels. 'We take two bricks, one in each hand. We place one on one side of the camel's testicles. The other brick we place on the other side. With one swift movement we bring the two bricks together, so. The camel is instantly castrated.' 'But doesn't it hurt?' 'No,' said the camel castrator, 'just so long as you make sure your fingers aren't near the edge!'

The story illustrates how the system is designed for the comfort of the people providing the service. The effect on the people receiving the service never enters the equation.

The mental health services of this country are narcissistic!!!

Jonathan is a manic-depressive. Both his Father and Grandfather were manic-depressives and they both died in the Maudslay Hospital in London. I am very proud to say I have been a friend of Jonathan. Not a great friend, not even a good friend. I am perhaps his only friend. He cut himself off from his family and even from Kathy who he met in hospital and who married him in prison. But what has my friendship with him, such as it is, got to do with finding your true self?

The signs along a Motorway are huge. They are sometimes lit. They are often luminous. But, it's astonishing how easy it is to miss them. The signs along life's journey are very similar. When you realise they're there then it's hard to miss them. But often we don't see them. Often they are hidden and so well hidden we pass them by.

There was Peter, my friend at University. There was Adam, the solicitor who got lost in the detail, there was Fred, being robbed and with no voice. All these people were signs. 'Turn again Dick', and turn again did Dick Whittington just as he was about to leave. He turned back and became Lord Mayor of London. Luckily his cat wasn't taken away by a man in a white coat in a white van! Knowing all these people should have caused me to ask myself, 'what is it all about, what's the point, where are you going, why are you going where you're going, who are you? Why do you have the dreams you have? Why are you so angry? Why can't you get angry?

So little dick just had to read the signs and turn. 'I took the road less travelled by and that has made all the difference.' Life presents us all with choices. I always think that with any choice, you may as well toss a coin, because you never have much of the relevant information to enable you to make an intelligent decision. We usually take the easy option, the road less travelled by and that makes all the difference. I had gone with the flow, not questioning whether I'd got it right or wrong. All the time there were voices telling me to 'turn again dick.' There were the dreams. There were the people I met along the way. And there was Jonathan. The story of Jonathan is the story of how your mind, your conscious mind, is a very dangerous thing, and a very unreliable thing. More than that, it's the story of how ultimately it's hard to find the help you need, and sometimes it's impossible. You don't even know who your friends are. Ultimately you have to take responsibility for your own life, because you're just a pawn in other people's lives if you don't.

Jonathan had been an engineer in the Navy and had ended up living in Northern Ireland. He was highly intelligent and his mind was a very powerful thing. He wrote a pamphlet condemning the IRA, which is something you didn't do in Northern Ireland at the time. Not unless you wanted to make some seriously unpleasant enemies.

He had a teenage daughter form a short-lived relationship and he was living with her and some other people in a house in Belfast.

One day he was arrested and charged with the rape of his daughter. If you have manic depression you can never be sure what you might have done or when you might have done it. He did know that his daughter had never mentioned this alleged incident to him and it was strange that all this was happening to him. His only defence could be that he was mentally ill, so that was his defence. Had he been properly advised he should have pleaded not guilty and tried to let them prove his guilt.

He was sentenced to a stay in Northern Ireland's Psychiatric Prison Maghaberry. He could be released if a cure could be found but for manic depression, there is no cure. If your daughter says you raped her than you can't imagine that she wouldn't be telling the truth. You believe her and the Court believes her.

Using the diminished responsibility defence is in one way a mistake as it gives rise to a verdict against which there is no Appeal and a sentence to which there is no end. On the other hand it did ensure that he was given much better medical treatment than he would have received in the NHS. He must have been inside for at least 15 years at the time of writing, which is about three times as long as you would get for rape. Had he not been in prison it's doubtful whether he would have survived. But who is to say he wouldn't be better off dead? What quality of life does he have? What sort of life did Fred have? What's the point? Tell me. What is the point?

Shortly after the trial, where the only evidence against him was that of his daughter, she suddenly acquired ownership of a new car and disappeared off on an expensive foreign holiday. It's almost certain that she'd been 'paid' to give evidence against him and that he was entirely innocent of any wrongdoing. His only crime was being ill. And having an illness that the Doctors were incapable of treating properly or at all.

Jonathan had been thrown out of the psychiatric hospitals he'd been admitted to before he'd been imprisoned. One incident is very telling. He had been found with alcohol, which had been forbidden. Ward rules. No alcohol. If you're in hospital with liver disease due to a lifetime of alcoholism do they throw you out if you're found with a tot of whisky in you locker, or if you break 'ward rules?' They don't and there would be an outcry if they did.

Now no one could tell Jonathan what he needed and what he didn't need. 'We self medicate,' was his expression, which I have never forgotten. It's a brilliant concept. And, yes, don't we all? If we need a drink we take one. If we need a paracetemol we have one. If a manic-depressive needs a whisky he has one. But breaking the rules is not something the mentally ill can do and he was discharged from hospital. By 'discharged' I mean he was placed at a bus stop outside the hospital, not knowing where he was, who he was, where 'home' was, or how he would get there. He was in all senses of the word, 'lost.'

If the mentally ill fail to co-operate with the hospital they are designated as suffering from personality disorders which can't be treated and then they are discharged. Co-operating with the hospital and obeying 'ward rules' is something you can only do if you are totally sane so almost by definition the ill are excluded from treatment and the sane are treated with whatever medication the Doctors feel like trying. If you respond to anti-depressants then you're suffering from depression. If you respond to drugs designed for schizophrenics then you're suffering from schizophrenia. If you fail to respond to any drugs you are suffering from a personality disorder and they discharge you.

There is something very symbolic about Jonathan's story. Mental illness can be like a prison sentence. There is no appeal. And there is no end, no release. It wasn't Jonathan that was guilty of a crime it was the system that so called 'sane' people, doctors have created. Many of us think that the patients have taken over the asylum!

The treatment of the mentally ill is like a cruel game. Fred survived a lifetime in a psychiatric hospital because he was totally sane. Had he been mentally ill, I can't imagine how he would have managed. Jonathan survives because he was imprisoned for a crime he didn't commit. Had he actually raped his daughter he would have served his sentence a long time ago and be on the scrap heap of this country's mental health services.

In a little terraced house in Nelson Road Ipswich lives a distant cousin of the Queen. Yes, that Queen. His name is Julian and I was privileged to meet him on several occasions. When Prince Charles and Lady Diana married he even received an invitation to the wedding. He didn't go. When I met him many years later he was blind and completely housebound. Like Jonathan, he too had served in the Navy as an engineer. He'd suffered from depression and when in Australia he'd been admitted to a Psychiatric Hospital and received ECT treatment, otherwise known as electric shock treatment. He blamed it for all his subsequent problems, which were enormous. He'd campaigned throughout his life for some justice for himself and thousand like him. I did some research through an Internet forum used by American Lawyers to see if there had ever been a case of medical negligence with the use of ECT. Even in California, the most litigious place in the world there was no record of any such claim being successful. There's a Catch 22 about being mentally ill and your testimony being fatally flawed as a result.

A neighbour who is sent money by Julian's family looks after Julian. His quality of life is minimal but at least he's not an embarrassment to his distinguished relatives.

It all goes to show that Society is a place where we have to conform to survive. If you don't conform, like my Grandad, like Jonathan you're as likely to be imprisoned. There is huge pressure to be what Society expects you to be, or in Peter's case, to be what your parents expect you to be. I conformed to what was expected of me. I believed what I was taught to be true. I tried to be what I thought was the right thing to be. I tried to be kind, to be like Jesus. That way I hoped to find the love that had been denied to me. It didn't work. People just take what they want and give nothing back. You give and receive nothing in return. You are used and the entire effort is counterproductive. If people do show you love and kindness it's hard to recognise it. You end up destroying yourself. You end up being crucified.

But I wasn't being true to myself. The self that was being destroyed wasn't my true self. I wasn't being me. Little Dick was lost, buried, with no place in the real world. He entered the world but was ignored and left to fade away. He needed rebuilding rediscovering. He needed to have his dog back. He needed to be loved and that's true of us all. In fact it's the only thing that matters. And if you want to be a sheep farmer in New Zealand then someone should say, 'good for you, do it.'

The dreams were telling me this. They were like great signs on the motorway. Turn again dick!

I once spent some time with a Lady who suffered from depression. I wrote this poem for her. It tries to show that we are all on a journey and however black the world seems we have to carry on. There's no point stopping and giving up. It's hard to think that though when you're down.

STEPPING STONES

Life is a series of stepping stones
We leave the river bank, kind hands guide us along the way.
The steps are small, the water shallow. Before long we are on our own.
The steps are far apart, the river becomes
Fast and deep. Sometimes the river is wide, sometimes just a single step.
Sometimes we move on by ourselves, sometimes we are moved against our will.
Sometimes we stay too long.
The light becomes dark. We can't find our way.
The blackness envelopes us. There seems no way to turn.
We must leap into the dark and trust the next stone is there.
As we reach the other side the stepping stones come to an end, our journey is nearly over.
The river bank is hidden from view but it's surely there as we take the final step.
The river flows. Others follow on. And we look back at the stepping stones. Each one leads us home.
Stepping Stones.
Stepping stones

When I was 11 years old I was taken ill with appendicitis. Strange though it seems nowadays, the surgeon came to our house to confirm the diagnosis. I think he had a Rolls Royce. It was a bit like the man coming to take away our dog.

Having examined me it was arranged that I would be taken in the next day for an emergency operation. The hospital was run by Irish nuns and was the same place I'd been born. It was named after the patron Saint of the Order St Francis. The nun who took care of me was a delightful person called Sister Dymphnah.

When I came round from the anaesthetic after the operation I remember opening my eyes and seeing my Mother and Father standing in the door. It's hard for even me to imagine it now but I shall never forget thinking, 'oh my God no.' I closed my eyes and pretended to be asleep hoping they would go away which they did.

Many years later I discovered that Dymphnah is not only the patron Saint of the mentally ill, but that there is also a place in Belgium named after her, (or is it him?') Each year at Dymphnah they hold a festival where the mentally ill are released from hospital and taken to Dymphnah for a 'cure,' rather like they do with the physically ill at Lourdes. The inhabitants of Dymphnah take people into their homes and care for them. Over the years there have been some remarkable cures. It is 'care in and by the community.' And it really works.

The point is that if we 'care' for people they are more likely to respond than if we take care of them. Sadly, society isn't yet prepared to do that although some individuals are. Thankfully.

A person who had a great effect on me throughout my life was my cousin Joan. She showed in her life, that a person caring for another person is what it's all about. It's effective. It works. Had she been born in the modern world she would probably have been treated as seriously mentally ill and placed on various medications to alleviate her "suffering.'

She was of my father's generation and he was very fond her. She had written two published novels and was therefore in my family's terms, a celebrity. Joan worked as a civil servant in London. Export Credits. There she met Clifford and fell in love. He, however, was married. His wife had multiple sclerosis. They both spent their entire working lives working for the same employer in the same office. Something that would never happen today. Clifford was an entertaining character. He once told me that there was no pay packet as good as your first pay packet. It's the only one that isn't spent before you receive it. How true that is!

Joan lived in a flat in East End Road East Finchley. Clifford had a house in Harrow. As his wife's illness deteriorated Joan moved in...to nurse Clifford's wife, which she did until she died several years later. They then were married. She became Mrs Rivers. Joan Rivers! No relation and not as funny!

Having moved to London after leaving University, Vanda and I were living in a bedsit in Tottenham. It was pretty gruesome but better than my digs at College! My Father wrote to me that Joan couldn't find a Buyer for the flat and so she would sell it to me for £5000. He had spoken to a friend of his, who was the local Manager of the Leicester Permanent Building Society and all I had to do was go and see the Manager of the branch in London. There was only one and it was in Park Lane!

It was a bit like Holy Joe wanting me to go to Cambridge. There was one major snag. I didn't have the basic qualifications. I didn't have a job! I was still at the College of Law. I had no income. Great idea, but how to achieve it!

I went anyway for the interview. Nothing to lose. Everything to gain. Park Lane and me as poor as a church mouse.

My file was marked, 'Preferential Applicant.' It was a promising start. 'So you aren't employed at the moment but you will be employed after you leave the College of Law?' 'Correct,' 'Well, that all seems in order.' Mortgage approved. I didn't tell him that Travers Smith would only take me if I passed my Law Finals and that I had failed miserably all the test papers I'd been set in preparation!
Yet again I had the feeling I was travelling under false pretences.

Joan's flat was quite a boost. And by some fluke I passed the exams! Three years later we sold the flat for about £15000!

Joan and Clifford eventually retired to Suffolk. To Oulton Broad. Here 25 years on, our paths crossed again. She became a regular listen to 'Thought for the Day' and gave me some welcome feedback, which was another boost. More importantly she helped me retrace the steps of my childhood and provided a window into the world of my Father's family before I was born. She helped me understand a little of why my Mother was the way she was and why the family treated her the way she did. Another sign along life's motorway.

In her Will she left me a 'copper kettle and trivet.' I was very grateful but it was as nothing to the tremendous legacy she gave me, not mentioned in her Will!

The strange thing about Joan, which I never knew till shortly before she died, was that she had a serious medical condition, which meant she was unable to eat! She lived on Complan, a powdered product given to the elderly you mixed with milk and drank. The Doctors thought she had a 'constricted throat,' which was too narrow to take solid food. Other Doctors thought it was psychological. Today she would have been regarded as anorexic and treated with whatever medication was in vogue at whatever 'unit' she'd have been sent. She was lucky that she was allowed to be the way she was and nobody sought to change her. She wasn't given a label. If you can't eat or don't want to eat what's the problem with that? She was happy to be the way she was!

Her funeral service was held at her Church, the Baptist Chapel in Oulton. It was my first ever encounter with the dreaded Chapel. It was everything I thought it might be and far worse! Real Bible bashing stuff. Sickening really but whatever turns you on….

I should mention that Joan too, suffered from a parental name change. She told me that her Mother, one day on a whim, announced to her and her brother, 'I'm tired of your names, I'm going to change them.' So Joan became 'Janey,' which is how she's known to her family!

Her brother Phil was a War hero, yes, even my family had one! He piloted a Lancaster bomber, a member of the famous 'Pathfinder' squadron. He was eventually shot down and put into a prisoner of war camp. He became very ill, so ill, that he was repatriated. My Father told a chilling story about how Phil was at a railway station on his way home across Germany. Half dead, and really too ill to make such a long journey home. The Germans never repatriated anyone who was likely to live long enough to recover and rejoin the war effort.

He was under armed guard but an officer of the Gestapo appeared on the platform, saw Phil and his RAF uniform, and drew out his pistol from it's holster. He sauntered up to Phil but his guards headed him off and somehow persuaded him to leave him alone.

I can't remember what Phil's name was changed to!

The camel castrator's bricks caught Jonathan where it hurts and continue to do so. Fortunately Joan escaped!

Was it a coincidence that I should fall in love with an Irish nun called Dymphnah and that Dymphnah was the patron Saint of the mentally ill? I stopped believing in coincidences!

CHAPTER 13 SHE DIES

My Mother lay dying in the Intensive Care Unit in Leicester Royal Infirmary. I was alone with her, and from nowhere, I was engulfed in the most desperate sadness I had known. I howled and howled with the terrible pain I felt. I had never cried like that before. Big boys don't. I sensed the curtains being pulled around us as I sobbed uncontrollably. I found myself saying these words as she lay, 'I love you Mother, you've been the most wonderful Mother in the world.' Not a single word was true but right until the very end I had to say what I thought would make her happy. I couldn't say what I really felt, 'you've hurt me more than any child should have been hurt and you never noticed.' It was a moment that told me a lot about the state I was in and the cliff edge I was heading to.

As my mother lay dying
I told her I loved her
That she'd been a good mother.
Of course it wasn't true.

But I'd spent my life trying to please her
So why stop now?

As my mother lay dying
I should have told her
How much she had hurt me
But I couldn't say what was true.

She spent her life in a mood
With me with my dad with everyone she knew.

As my mother lay dying
I wept tears like never before
Tears for the childhood
When I felt so alone.

Tears for a lifetime trying to be good
So why stop now?

My mother lives on in the pain
And the grief that I feel,
For a life never lived
Words that were never true.

And one day, will I lay dying
Still feeling alone?
And hoping to be free at last
From this lifetime of pain.

She was fighting to stay alive but I knew she was never going to regain consciousness, that it was time for her to die. I felt she could hear me, as she seemed to respond, so I said, 'Dad's here waiting for you.' I felt she would understand as she believed that when she died she would see him again and also the children she lost as miscarriages and stillborn. She needed to know that her time had come. She wasn't going to get better. She had to move on to wherever she was going. I just had to tell her. No one else would. No one else had the guts. No one else understood her like I did. Not even my brother. Just wait for her to struggle on? You wouldn't do that to a dog. No, you'd pick them up and help them on the way. I was the man in the white coat. The van was waiting.

There was nothing. Just her laboured breathing as she struggled on. I tried again. 'Richard's here.' She responded immediately. She suddenly opened her eyes then closed them for the very last time and after a short while she passed away.

Dad didn't like being kept waiting. I entered into her world of spirits, life after death and all that cranky stuff she lived and breathed. I had no idea whether he was there or not. But again, it was what she would have wanted to hear.

I'd had a similar experience some years before with an old lady who was waiting to die. She was really worried about being alone. 'Will you be with me?' She asked. 'No, I won't be with you but your Mother and Father will come for you,' 'But they're dead!' 'Yes, but they'll be with you.' She passed away peacefully that same night. She just needed to know she wouldn't be alone. I still have the family Bible she gave me. On her mantelpiece was a picture of a young RAF pilot. It was her 'young man.' He was on a training flight over the Suffolk Coast and never returned. She could have been angry, but she never showed it if she was. After 50 years I suppose you accept it. Well, at least some do.

As we drove away from my Mother's house for the very last time, again the tears and sadness overwhelmed me. For about thirty seconds, no more than that. I had never before cried like this. I knew, or thought I knew, that I would never now feel the love that a child should not only feel but should grow up with. Should be enriched by. Should be swamped by. The love I make sure, as best I can, that my children feel. The love that all parents should try to make their children feel. There was now an emptiness. A void. Perhaps there always had been.

At her funeral I knew that I had to deliver an address. I knew it was what she would have wanted. I knew I had to 'show off' myself in front of her friends. She would be there, in spirit, basking in the glory of her son who went to Cambridge, delivering a brilliant epitaph. A 'thought for the day' She would love it but for one more time she wouldn't be able to tell me. She wouldn't' be able to say 'well done, that was brilliant.' I would do my best but despite the promise she made when I went off to take my 11 plus exam, my best wouldn't be good enough. I shall never forget looking down at my three beautiful daughters, whist I was up there speaking, and seeing their sad eyes all filled with tears. I later asked them why they were crying because none of them was close to her. 'It was because you were sad.' They said as one. I kept going and finished it. The last thing I was to do for her. They all said it was brilliant but again that meant nothing to me. I needed my Mother to be proud of me, to love me, but yet again, that love, that pride was missing. I was asked by my nephew to throw some earth onto her coffin as it was lowered into the ground. I couldn't do it. I'd done enough.

Look at the words I used in that paragraph, 'I knew, I knew, I knew.' I never use the words, 'I felt.' I had to ask my daughters why they were sad. Why didn't I know?

My sister in law pointed out that I had mentioned in my speech her visiting New Zealand, which I thought she had but in fact she hadn't. It was fitting that for one last time I hadn't quite got it right.

Children ask thousands of questions, some inconsequential some of major importance. Many aren't easy to answer mainly because we've never answered them for ourselves.

Here's a poem I wrote that expresses this and tries to provide answers to the important questions,

Questions children ask

Daddy, why are fire engines all called Dennis? And
Daddy, why can't he British win at tennis? And
Daddy, why do ladies talk too much,
And when they do it's double dutch?
And Daddy, where did Grandad go when he died?
And why was Nanna so sad she cried? And
Daddy where was I before I was born? And
Daddy, why do you have to mow the lawn?

Well, the fireman's engines are made by Dennis,
And if we cared enough we'd win at tennis.
Ladies talk because men don't hear.
Nanna's sad because a life alone she fears.

And when Grandad died he lived on in you.

And Joseph, where's your other shoe?
And before you were born?

You were in the love of Mummy and me.

The only question I could never answer is why my Father seemed to spend his entire day off mowing the lawn but I think I'm beginning to understand a little now.

Motorways have those great big signs suspended over them warning of a junction ahead. I now had what I needed to tell me that Steve got it wrong. It was time to find Little Dick. First exit, over the bridge and back along life's highway, retracing the steps. It hadn't been a wasted journey. There had been much to enjoy, some success, some very good times, some wonderful memories. The kitchen and the drama that unfolded there. Like Mary Poppins. It would be a long journey back, revisiting the times and places I stopped at on the journey down. It was getting lighter and the traffic wasn't half as bad going the other way. At times I thought I'd never make it. Too much water had passed under the bridge. Just to end up where you started. Little Dick, I'm coming to get you! A medium once told me that we choose to be born into the families we are born into. We choose the sort of lives we have because there are particular lessons we need to learn. If we don't learn them we have to come back, reborn in another family, just as bad or just as good to try again and again until we learn enough to move on. To another life to learn another lesson. Sometimes if we've had an easy life we'll choose a hard one next time.

Most of all, we are reborn to renew the love we've had in previous lives. We have to rediscover those souls we've loved before. When we meet again those special souls we've known before, we instantly hit it off. There's an overwhelming feeling that this person is the right one. It's like coming home. The chemistry is there. It's like we've always known each other. And indeed we have and for longer than we realize.

We certainly learn more from the suffering we have. Without it we probably learn nothing and what a waste that is. It seems to me that all the mental health problems we have are gifts, to make us retrace our steps. Signs along the motorway telling us to think about it. Maybe the dreams we have say the same. Maybe the memories we have are there for a reason, if only we can unravel them all. It's a pity not too! We may have to live this life all over again and wouldn't that be just too miserable. Not me chum! Not me! Little dick's gonna sort it out!

Many years ago when I was young there was an Olympic High Diver called Brian Phelps. He gained a silver medal, if I remember the story correctly. To win a gold medal he had to unlearn all his diving he'd ever learned to correct a fault in his run up. The TV showed him practicing the most basic parts of diving. As far as I know he never had any more success as a diver and I often wondered why I remembered the story. But it shows that if you've got something wrong when you start out the only way is to go back and correct it. Ask any Golfer. No don't. They're too boring.

A SHORT POEM

You miss them when they're gone,
Your Mum and Dad.
At simple times like mowing the lawn
Like he did on those Sundays long ago.
Standing in the sunlight, fag in hand.
A solitary man.

You miss them when they're gone
Your Mum and Dad.
Swimming lengths in the pool
Like she did, now so long ago.
Fighting against the years,
The stiffness, the painful joints
The widowhood those lonely years.

You miss them when they're gone
Your Mum and Dad.
Just memories now so, so long ago.
A childhood gone forever
But love remains. A bond uniting
Beyond the grave.

You miss them when they're gone
Your Mum and your Dad.

Much of what I've been saying tells you what I thought. Not much tells you what I felt. I have difficulty dealing with feelings. I don't have the capacity to easily recall feelings. I had a huge capacity to feel but a limited capacity to express it. It made me think I probably didn't feel much. Whatever I felt, I didn't thing mattered. What mattered was making my Mother happy and if I ever did that, I never knew it, because she couldn't show it. Why she couldn't show it I'll never know. What made her the way she was, I'll never know. Part of finding little Dick was to tell him that it wasn't his fault. He did his best but it wasn't his responsibility. He was the child, she was the parent. Sadly, she got it wrong. Many of us do but I don't have to make excuses for her. I just have to discover the pain I never allowed myself to feel. It's OK to feel angry. It's OK to feel sadness for a childhood lost. It's never too late to retrace your steps, to take another path. Learning how to feel isn't easy, learning how to express your feelings is even harder.

The main feeling I have is of being defeated. Wishing I was dead. The word I always use, 'defeated,' is an interesting one. It shows I see myself in a battle. I see myself as trying in vain to win. Always failing. Never feeling I've scored a point let alone winning the battle. Defeated. Who is the enemy? How would I recognize a victory?

The battle is in striving to be loved, to be noticed. To have my feelings recognized. This is a battle I can never win. Once a narcissist always a narcissist, and then she dies. The final defeat. Game over. I lost.

It's strange how whenever I am involved in a game, be it scrabble, monopoly, watching football, I have to win at all costs. Yet I get no satisfaction from winning. I finish a marathon and people talk of the feeling of elation. I never did. I always feel....you guessed it, defeated. Could have done better. Tried hard but lost. Even at school, we had marks for every week, every term, every year, every exam and at the end of the school year they were all added up and I so desperately wanted to come first. I never did, but why did it matter? It mattered because I would have loved to go home and to tell my Mother I had won, and then for her to have been pleased. I now know she never would have been pleased. She would have been pleased for herself, for her reflected glory, 'my son did well,' but she couldn't have been pleased for me.

But the little dick in me has to believe he can do it, he really can. He has no optimism, no belief that the world around will ever change. He has to learn optimism. He has to experience the world changing. He's allowed himself to be a slave for so long. A slave to other people's needs. Trying to be good, trying to be kind, never once thinking of himself. Never once feeling that he deserved better than this. Those two white people took away his running shoes but he's getting them back, he really is. Well done dick! If others can't tell him I can! You're a great success and you're writing a great book.

CHAPTER 14   FINDING DICK

You can't beat driving over a cliff and crashing on the beach below for making you realise you've been going in the wrong direction! When you reach that point there's really nowhere else to go. No scrambling back up the cliff just to throw yourself off again. As the tide approaches you really know you're at a turning point, with limited options.

My personal crash came one day a few years ago when the phone rang. It was Neil, a Solicitor friend with a criminal practice to tell me that a client of mine, who was being investigated for fraud, had told the police that I'd either put him up to it, or I'd given him the idea. That's to say, when you're caught red handed all you can say is, 'it wasn't me guv, it was him over there, he told me to do it.' I managed to put down the phone, but I passed out, stone cold, out! I became aware that my small office was filled with four ambulance men! How many do they send when someone's really injured! Must have been a quiet day. But why am I making a joke of this? Why do I have to mask my pain with light-hearted banter? Am I pretending nothing's wrong because I'm ashamed or because deep down I can't bear to be a failure, to be seen as a failure, to upset you, anyone, my Mother, because the only time I was ever noticed was when I did well at something? And even then I never quite did well enough, not even getting a 2.1 degree at Cambridge. 'You didn't let her beat you did you?'

The ambulance people wanted to whisk me off to Hospital, but I'd done that and got the shorts and the T-shirt. I had to sign two forms. There are only two reasons why they can allow you not to go to Hospital. If you sign a disclaimer, or if you're dead. I signed the disclaimer although I was as good as dead.

So how was I to survive this? I had faced losing my family when I was divorced. I had faced losing my career when I lost my partnership. Now I faced all of that and faced being sent to prison. It's a lingering death at the cliff face. Nothing happens very suddenly. For days, weeks, months, years you wait, hearing nothing. Waiting for a knock at the door. Waiting for a phone call. Waiting for a letter. First stop was back to the doctor for the magic pills. For once in my life a Doctor was kind and caring. Try the worst case scenario. Christmas in an open prison. Could be better than this living death. Try the pills. They were like having a small ladder when you're trying to climb a cliff. At least the ladder may keep your head above the rising tide apart from the occasional breaking wave! And there I go again trying to be cheery. Taking my own life was a best case scenario. But, as the Medium said, maybe I'd be sent back to go through it all again, and again, until I learned the lesson. What lesson?

You have to carry on working. You and your family have to eat. How do you keep going when you have all that hanging over you? The actor on the stage again. Cheery Steve, always a merry quip to lighten other people's load. Pretending it's not happening. I needed someone to talk to. There was always God, 'Lord Jesus Christ, Son of the Living God, have mercy on me a sinner.' It helped. Going to Church helped. If I'd brought this on myself, if I was being punished, I could beg forgiveness, say I was sorry. For the first time in my life I asked for help. On the Internet I searched for a counsellor, maybe counselling would help. Please God, not a grey haired do-gooding lady earning some pin money and making herself feel better in the process. I found two names. I rang the first one, no reply, try the next one, a kindly northern voice answered and agreed to see me a few days later. I carried on doing the Morning Thought, trying to help others and all the time not waving but drowning.

The fraud squad officers told me they wanted to interview me. A taped interview. I knew a little about how they work. They gather information, sometimes it takes years, and when the investigation's complete they make the arrest. With ordinary criminal investigations the arrest comes first. You know what you're up against. Here the enemy was sinister and deeply threatening. I had no idea what the client was involved in, no idea how he was trying to implicate me. Like playing chess when you can't see your opponent's pieces. My only crumb of comfort was that I knew I had done nothing wrong. I knew I was innocent, but often that isn't enough. I took a Solicitor with me, Craig a friend from times gone by, and I shall be eternally grateful to him for that. I have no real friends in the legal community. Maybe they think I'm a dangerous maverick. I certainly don't fit in with their cosy Masonic groupings.

I answered all their questions and they assured us I was there only as a witness. This wasn't true and I later found out they were compiling a case against me. The Law Society were advised of the investigation and also the Local Law Society. Everyone knew but nobody said a word.

The sleepless nights were terrible. I said over and over again, 'Lord Jesus Christ, Son of the Living God, have mercy on me a sinner.' It seemed to help, better than the awake nightmare my mind created for me. Better to get up and read a paper, but desperately tired, desperate for some respite from the torture I was suffering. All the time keeping a brave face at work as if nothing was happening.

I was out of the office one morning having my photo taken for some publicity that the firm was planning, and whilst I was out three members of the Suffolk Constabulary arrived at the office, accompanied by the most senior member of the Law Society investigations team. They had a High Court Order requiring the production and removal of files. I tried to open a conversation with them but they were having none of it. Away they went but now the story was out and I sensed a rumour spreading like gossip always does. It's such fun for people who have little else in their lives. 'Stigma' is a word, which comes nowhere near describing how it is to have the world thinking badly about you. You are totally destroyed as a person, your self-respect is in tatters, and if you wished you were dead before, you really wish it now.

They took the files away and the man from the Law Society announced that they would be coming back to undertake a thorough investigation of my work. It would be unlimited in it's scope. I knew my career was at an end and a reputation and expertise built up over thirty years was gone. The clients, the families, the friends I'd been involved in were lost, dead and buried. I never cried, maybe having no feelings was a help. Maybe crying would have helped, in fact, I'm sure it would. Big boys don't cry but they really should. People would then know how frightened they were.

I have always been frightened of being lonely. As I found at meal times at University, you could be the loneliest when you were with people, especially if they knew each other and you knew nobody. That was hard. Being on your own isn't lonely, that's easy. Being 'out' and on your own, now that's lonely. I was now very lonely. With the world talking about me. As the Americans say, 'dead man walking.'

The kindly lady with the Northern accent was Annee, and what a fantastic person she turned out to be. We laughed together, cried together, we set out on the journey together to find little dick. We got the show on the road, a better road, perhaps the right road, away from the cliff. We stumbled, we walked, we strolled, we sauntered but we were making progress. Each week I had to promise not to take my own life before we were to meet the following week, or if I felt I wasn't going to make it, I had to promise to ring her. I joked that I paid someone every week to tell me I was a good person, and at times that, was all I needed to hear.

My weekly appointment with Annee was literally a lifeline. It was like being given a lifeboat to take me off the beach. She told me I had a black crow sitting on my shoulder telling me that the worst was about to happen. The black crow was my Father telling me I'd never get in to Cambridge. She gave me a wooden stick to beat it with which I carried around in my car. Sometimes she cried at the sadness of it all, even though I couldn't cry myself. Where were my feelings in all of this? Just the same old feeling of defeat.

She once asked me if she reminded me of my Mother. From nowhere I burst into tears, 'I just wish my Mother had been like you.' I sobbed and sobbed. I hadn't thought it before, hadn't felt it, but now I did, and golly, how it hurt. How it hurt. But at least I was learning to express my feelings. She tried to teach me how to get angry. To beat a pillow with a baseball bat. She'd had to learn it too. I found it very hard. Anger is something I hadn't expressed before. Being married for twelve years without a hug, without a kiss, without an 'I love you,' had made me angry but I could never express it. To such an extent that I doubted I had the capacity to feel anything at all. If I had expressed some of my feelings maybe I could found an answer. Maybe I could have been a father to my daughter. Lots of 'maybes.'

She got me thinking about what else I might do, sheep farming in New Zealand was probably out of the question, but I thought about going in for teaching. It had been my plan B when I lost my partnership. It gave me something to look forward to when the shit hit the fan. My Mother had done it so maybe it was in the blood. I made an application through UCAS and went for an interview at Homerton College Cambridge. I was even accepted although I could never quite see myself teaching. The awesome responsibility of young people's lives and exam results seemed far too great. I don't imagine teachers see it like that but I did. The people at Homerton really wanted me to do it and were very encouraging. If only they had known the real reason why I was applying!

So, my plan B was in place and the weeks and months ticked by. The Law Society inspection was unbelievably humiliating. Imagine working in an office of 70 people and everyone knowing that the stranger poking his nose round the place was looking for wrong doing by you, one of the owners of the firm. My counselling touched on why this sequence of life threatening disasters might keep happening. Did I sub-consciously let it happen or even make it happen and if I did why? Maybe I'm too emotionally damaged to have a position of responsibility. Maybe I feel it's all a dreadful mistake and I don't deserve any of the success I've had. When you spend your life wishing you were dead then you don't have the energy to protect your back as you should. You don't have the attention to detail you should have. You don't care. Caring is a feeling you aren't capable of. Maybe I'd given up hope of ever feeling loved or worthy of being loved. The effort of simply carrying on, battling away and always feeling defeated makes life just about impossible. Perhaps destroying my professional and personal life was the only cry for help that I could manage without actually killing myself. Strangely enough, now I had cried for help, and the help had come. They were taking my dog away and I was now crying with the sadness of it all.

Little by little, I discovered or rather uncovered, little dick, the person I might have been. He might have been a teacher, if only someone had believed he could do it. Maybe he could have had a career in Theology, if only he had a little self-belief. Maybe he should have stayed at Travers Smith, if only he'd some insight into his real abilities. Maybe he could have been a good husband, if only. Many, 'if onlys.' I had to travel back along the road I'd come to see why I'd made the decisions I'd made. I had to rebuild the house that had fallen into disrepair.

On Radio, I carried on with the Morning Thoughts. It's called, keeping up appearances. I could say to the world, 'if you think I'm dead then you're wrong.' If Steve was dead and buried then little dick was about to make a comeback!

I couldn't imagine I hadn't broken some rule somewhere, mainly because I didn't know half the rules, you just can't, and they make them up as they go along anyway. 'Professional Misconduct,' can mean whatever they want it to mean. It's like driving down the road being followed by a police car. Were your tyres OK, do your lights work, were you speeding? Looked at later, an innocent set of circumstances can look quite different to how they looked at the time. Day after day the inspection ground on, grinding me deeper into the dust, saying nothing, just making notes. And then, he went. Nothing, not a word except to someone else saying that there was going to be no further action taken. And the police? Many months later I had a call telling me that there would be no action taken. Thanks a lot. About two years of my life destroyed. My mental health destroyed. The occasional optimism that takes most people through life, destroyed. Steve destroyed but little dick? What did I feel? I now have to keep asking myself that. Relief? Just nothing, no feelings. Yet another marathon, and no feelings, just the certain knowledge that the real problem was how I'd arrived there in the first place. How I'd missed all the signs. How I'd gone over the cliff and how I was going to heal the wound, stop the eternal endless suffering, stop wishing I was dead, start looking forward. Go back down the road, find my running shoe, find little dick. Get a dog.

Annee taught me about Narcissism. Her Mother had been one too. She understood how the little lad hadn't felt able to express his feelings, to cry out, 'look at me I'm hurting.' How his Mother's feelings were all that was important to him. How it wasn't his fault, his responsibility. He was the child, she was the parent. How being good and kind was the only way he knew to win the love he'd been denied. He not only had to be good and kind he had to be Jesus. He had to work miracles, to save people from themselves, from depression, from manic-depression. He had to be St Francis and have a close affinity with animals, birds, fish, all the beasts of the field. He had to get a First at Cambridge, had to be a radio star, had to be a real Solicitor. Maybe he had to write a book too. Like Cousin Joan. Be a famous writer. He could never be little dick, that wasn't interesting, he wasn't somebody a Mother could love, so I buried him and left the house that was dick's house to rot. I lost my running shoes.

I can't begin to imagine the horror of being raped but that's the only way I can describe what had happened to me. The horror of being raped must be as bad as the horror of living with the memory of it, going through it over and over again, day after day. But it had set me on a road to recreate a real person, a person who could feel, and a person who could say what he felt. An achievement greater than anything, if only I could do it. Sometimes I'm swamped by the hopelessness of it all, but that desperate low makes me pick myself up, dust myself down and start all over again. I often liken it to being asked to jump the high jump. It sounds perfectly straightforward. Bar, jump. Got it! But if you can jump three feet and the bar is six feet then even with all the encouragement and coaching in the world you ain't gonna make it. The strange thing is that the bar isn't always quite as high as you think it is. Sometimes it's just a hop!

15 THE LAST CHAPTER

She usually went to bed on her own and I followed up later, turning on my side and going to sleep. I needed to feel loved; I needed to express my love in return. I couldn't do it. I've never been able to do it. It was the fundamental part of living a fulfilled life, of being happy, and I couldn't do it. I had a failed marriage to prove it. I had a daughter who had to grow up without a Father because of it. I had failed business relationships. I had been perilously close to being imprisoned. It was dragging me down to the deepest depths of despair and I was powerless to do anything about it, being engulfed in a sense of hopelessness. Like standing in front of a house armed only with a j-cloth and needing to renovate the whole building. Where do you start? Or standing in front of a shallow grave desperate to turn back the clock and bring the body back to life. Standing at the start of a race with only one shoe. My way of dealing with things didn't work any longer. I no longer wanted to die. No plan B.

I wanted, and felt I deserved, to see my grandchildren born and take their place in the world. I wanted to collect conkers for them and buy them penguin biscuits. I could be a great Grandad, I know I could. I wanted to walk my three daughters down the aisle and see them happily married. I want to see my son enjoy the pride in his children that I have felt in mine. To watch his son score a goal, score a try, make a tackle and feel that amazing sense of pride. To see his son enjoy a relationship with his grandparents as my children have with theirs. I had every reason to hurl a hammer against the wall and make a huge hole. I never dared express my anger. Was never confident enough in my parents' feelings for me to do that.

It was up to me now. My 'child' had been hurt; my 'parent' had to take control. I was a good parent. I ought to be able to do it. For Christ's sake, all I had to do was to say not what I thought, but what I felt. And this time the feelings were very powerful. Being at rock bottom brings out the best in me. Somehow you have nothing to lose but life itself. As the Chinese saying goes, 'every crisis is an opportunity for change.' This was a crisis!

I went to put my hand on her side but this was greeted with a 'don't irritate me, you make me hot'. 'That's a good excuse', I said, and after a few minutes climbed out of bed, a strange feeling of intense anger mounting inside me. As I went to leave the room I found myself saying, 'if a husband can't touch his wife it's a poor thing'. That may not have sounded angry to you, but for me that was as angry as I could be. And anyway, I didn't have a hammer.

Downstairs I went, a fiercer anger rising inside of me. Several days passed, the anger growing and growing. Our wedding anniversary was coming up and there was no way I wanted to do the usual, flowers, card, present, meal, which is how we always celebrated our special day. At bedtime I stormed into the bedroom, got into bed and said many things I had always wanted to say but never felt able. I was then overwhelmed by a tidal wave of love, like the water released from a dam. There was no fight, no terrifying mood, no tears; we just lay in each other's arms surrounded by our love for each other.

For the first time in my life I was able to say what I felt without fear of being rejected. The feelings, that all my life I doubted I had, were there after all. Buried but not dead and buried. Like a dilapidated house that needed discovering and renovating. My feelings were not only valued, expressing them was a trigger releasing an outpouring of overwhelming love. A response I could never have imagined. My feelings had been there like an old fine wine in a bottle, corked and sealed with the label fallen off.

It had been a long journey of rediscovery. Retracing my steps. An ultra, extreme marathon. The house was now habitable, the roof repaired, the garden tidied, a sign on the gate, Little dick lives, and lives here. A place to escape from the asylum, a place to be yourself, not what you think others want you to be. A place to be loved. A place to be loving in return.

A few days later chipmunkapublishing released my 'words and music' on their website and the feeling of being valued, worth something, was amazing. Only £1 to download a track, not much, but twice as much as I had thought they were worth. Little dick was reborn. I received an e-mail telling me I'd sold my first CD. Look out Madonna, little dick is on his way to his first hit. (I can dream).

I was about to say that my Mother would have been so proud of me. That's what normal people would say, but my Mother, even if somewhere in her soul she could feel pride, would never have been able to express it, would never have been able to acknowledge the achievement except in bragging about it to her friends. I had created what I regarded as a new art form. Poetry read not with background music, but woven into the notes like the lyrics of a song, creating a rich tapestry of sounds, ideas, thoughts. And why would that have made her resentful, angry? She had to be at the centre of things, centre stage. The spotlight always had to shine on her. The applause had to be for her. The rave reviews. The autographs. The red carpet. The bouquets. I can hear her saying from the grave, 'I always thought he would.'

There never was a red carpet in her life apart from the reflected glory of her family. Nothing I did seemed to stop her anger, the sadness never left her, hurt by perhaps her Mother who never praised her, never offered her the love she needed. So one day she took a hammer in her frustration and heaved it at the wall, to say, 'look at me world, look at me Mother, see my pain.' And as the plaster came crashing down there was a sign, a sign which the world ignored. A sign that could never be plastered over.

Am I making excuses? Possibly, but I know she was a wonderful, powerful woman with a brilliant fierce mind. Damaged, doomed to a life of bitterness. And how common is that? And if she had been born today would she have turned to drugs, to drink, to blot out the pain, to bring a little happiness? Would she have self-harmed to release the pressure rising like a tide inside? And who could have blamed her if she had? Not for her a life of sympathy like the crippled Aunt Flo. Not for her the life of drowning your sorrows at the Kettering Working Mans Club like her Aunt Kate. Not for her, an early death asleep by the front door on a cold winter's night. Not for her an ignominious end in the children's boating lake at Wickstead Park.

I have to reflect that the man entitled to be bitter, angry, my Grandad never was. Or not as far as I know. He lost his Mother at the age of 7. Sent away to work at 13. Robbed of his life savings by a churchwarden he trusted. Imprisoned by his own Country. Tortured and humiliated in prison. Despised as a pawnbroker. Victim of an armed assault. And yet, a man of great tenderness and kindness. A man who'd give you his last penguin biscuit.

I would have liked to have loved my Mother and shared the warmth of a Mother's love but that was never to be. More than anything I needed to feel loved by her. But as a Father, I know, like all parents, how much our parents sacrificed for us, how much they loved us. But how much do we damage our children? Maybe it's not damage. Maybe it's a gift. Something to write a book about. Something to share with others. Something I was born to discover and recover from and so help others. Maybe I would have been sent back to live this life, again and again, until I learned the lesson.

The other day I bought a new toothbrush. Because my eyesight isn't what it was I bought by mistake, one with hard bristles. I normally have one with 'medium' bristles. My new brush is uncomfortable to use but it gets my teeth really clean. A soft brush would be the most comfortable but wouldn't clean half as well. Life is like that. Given the choice we'd never go for a hard life but how much more do we learn from the pain we suffer? A soft life would be comfortable but we'd gain little from it. I was thinking too about the pain of childbirth. How the midwives tell women to use the pain to push with. And with every pain they push the baby a little further out. The pain I've suffered in life is like that too. From every disaster I've wished I was dead but I've emerged wiser and stronger. I've discovered a little more about little dick. A friend who has suffered all her life from depression said the same. That the illness made her ask questions about herself in a way that nothing else could have done.

There may be someone in your life, a parent, a partner, a work colleague who is very charming, persuasive and successful, but who ultimately takes ruthlessly and gives nothing. Leaving you feeling abandoned and ruined. Whose words are far louder than their actions. Who leaves you feeling used. Leaves you thinking it was all your fault for being inadequate. You now know that you can stand up for yourself. That good will always conquers evil. You may have to be at rock bottom to bring about the changes but try you must. If I can do it so can you. It may be what your life is all about and if you don't do it you may be sent back to go through it all again until you do.

Thank you for listening. Thank you for caring enough to hear me. Thank you for helping me heal myself.

And I wonder what shall now be my dream? The other night I dreamed that the house had a little hole in the wall with a broken copper water pipe needing repair. Looking after yourself is an ongoing project you never finish. I still feel I shall be glad when it's all over.

We all are very loveable, however bad some of us feel about ourselves. We all have the capacity to love and to be loved and unless we fulfil that capacity it's as if we've never lived. Don't miss the point and get sent back to try again. God forbid!

P.S

My brother's family wouldn't allow him to read any of this. They said it would make him too angry. This somehow proves the point of what I've said. Someone who did read this was my friend Neil. He wrote this to me. 'I have read your book and I can tell that it was written from the heart. I empathise with nearly all you say and it really does portray what an awful world we live in. Right now I am facing the biggest challenge of my life. If anyone should be dead it is me because I am at the bottom of a big hole with no way of getting out of it. Like you and most other people, I crave to be loved and to be number one in someone's life. But your book has inspired me and for the moment you might have saved my life.'

Tragically he never posted that letter and a few days later he was found, hanged in his garage.

THE END